The Answer Is A Miracle

By Robert Perry and Allen Watson

#22 in a series based on *A Course in Miracles*

This is the twenty-second book in a series, each of which deals with the modern spiritual teaching *A Course in Miracles*. If you would like to receive future publications directly from the publisher, or if you would like to receive the newsletter that accompanies this series, please write us at the address below.

The Circle of Atonement
Teaching and Healing Center
P.O. Box 4238
West Sedona, AZ 86340
(520) 282-0790, Fax (520) 282-0523
E-mail: circleofa@sedona.net
Website: http://nen.sedona.net/circleofa/

The ideas presented herein are the personal interpretation and understanding of the authors, and are not necessarily endorsed by the copyright holder of *A Course in Miracles*: Foundation for Inner Peace, Inc., P.O. Box 598, Mill Valley, CA 94942.

Excerpts from *A Course in Miracles* Copyright © 1975. Reprinted by permission of Foundation for Inner Peace, Inc., P.O. Box 598, Mill Valley, CA 94942.

ISBN 1-886602-12-3

Published by The Circle of Atonement: Teaching and Healing Center
Printed in the United States of America

Cover design by Pakaage
Typesetting by Greg Mackie

Table of Contents

Introduction

A *Course in Miracles*. Its very title announces that its purpose is to teach us miracles. It wants to train us in the experience of miracles, so that they become completely natural for us. The very word "miracle" kindles feelings of hope. However one defines the word, it conveys a sense of instantaneous release from a problem that looked insoluble. It evokes an image of liberation that comes from beyond the strength of our little bodies and brains, from beyond the framework in which the problem seemed cemented in place. In a world full of problems, a world which is itself an interlocking grid of problems, who does not wish for a miracle?

The promise of miracles is exactly what has drawn so many of the Course's students to it. Yet the concept of miracles has become a major source of confusion for most Course students. So confusing has this topic become that many students can talk for hours about the Course and never even mention the word "miracle." It has simply dropped out of their picture of the Course. How can the very thing the Course is meant to teach us be absent from our picture of the Course? And how can we learn miracles unless that is an actual goal of ours, and unless we have some understanding of what miracles are?

This book is designed to help restore the concept of miracles to the center of the Course, where it belongs. It is designed, first of all, to impart a clear understanding of what miracles are. It also attempts to show the differences between miracle-minded thinking and our normal way of thinking, as well as to clarify the relationship between the Course's miracle and the traditional concept of the miracle. Its overall goal is to allow the reality of miracles to come back into our minds and permeate our thinking. Its goal is to lead us to a place where we see the frequent experience of miracles as entirely possible, as a true goal to which we aspire, and as the end toward which the Course is guiding us.

-1-
Defining the Miracle
by Allen

B y the end of this opening chapter, we hope to give a working definition of the word *miracle*, based on the Course. I will begin by walking us through different aspects of miracles as seen by the Course: the preparation for miracles; the context of miracles; the source of miracles; the interpersonal nature of miracles; and the results of miracles. As we look at each of these aspects we will see things that are associated with miracles but which are not the miracle itself. My hope is that as we get a clearer idea of what a miracle *is not*, the truth of what a miracle *is* will become clearer for us all. At the end of the chapter, Robert will give his summary definition of what a miracle really is.

Why is a miracle so hard to define?

Why is it that, although many of us have been reading and studying and practicing *A Course in Miracles* for years, we find it so hard to pin down the exact meaning of the word *miracle*?

The Course does not give a precise definition

The Course uses the words *miracle* or *miracles* 559 times. So our difficulty can't be that the Course doesn't say enough about miracles; it talks about them a lot. To most readers, it seems that, in talking about miracles, the Course dances around the word without ever really defining it. It makes comparisons that tell us what miracles are like; it tells us about their effects; it tells us of conditions for them. But it doesn't seem to tell us exactly what they are!

For instance, in one place the Course tells us: "A miracle is a correction introduced into false thinking by me [Jesus]" (T-1.I.37:1). That is actually one of the clearest definitions of *miracle* in the Course, and we will look at it more carefully later. Yet it isn't a very good definition: It really tells us more about what a miracle *does*—it corrects—than what it *is*. It's as if I have a severe case of some kind of flu, and the doctor tells me, "I have a treatment for this disease." When I ask what the treatment is, he tells me, "It cures the disease."

That isn't what we want to know, however. What we want to know, in the case of our flu, is: Exactly what is the treatment? Is it a pill I take? Is it a diet I

1

have to follow? Do I need a series of shots? Do I need to sit in a sauna for an hour a day and drink six quarts of water? Does someone lay hands on me and pray? Do I wear a crystal for a week? What *is* the treatment?

The Course seems to have a hard time answering that kind of question about what a miracle is. I remember the first time I read the section in the Workbook titled, "What Is a Miracle?" thinking, "Ah! At last, now I will find out exactly what a miracle is." But when I was done reading I was as unclear as ever! In this book, we hope to end that confusion. By the end of this chapter, we are going to give you a definition for the word *miracle* that, we hope, will satisfy us all, and be true to all that the Course has to say about miracles.

It is hard to define a miracle

Why is it, though, that a book called *A Course in Miracles*, that uses the word 559 times, seems to be so unclear about what they are? At least unclear *to us*; I think we would all agree that the author seems to know exactly what miracles are.

A good part of the reason, I think, is that a miracle is something completely alien to our normal way of thinking. We have, with our egos, constructed a very consistent and rigid view of the world and of reality. A miracle, by its very nature, represents the intrusion into this world view of a thought system that is diametrically opposed to that of the ego. The Course says:

> Since the miracle aims at restoring the awareness of reality, it would not be useful if it were bound by laws that govern the error it aims to correct (T-1.III.9:4).

So, since a miracle is simply not bound by the laws of this world, it is actually something so alien to our thinking that our minds have a terrible time getting a grasp on it. All our thinking tells us to try to define a miracle in terms of the laws of this world, of time, of space, of physicality, of doing things. And it can't be defined that way because it does not belong to this world. It is the intrusion of the laws of Heaven into this world, and it obeys only Heaven's laws.

So, perhaps we can begin to get an inkling of what a miracle is by realizing first what it is not: If our understanding of a miracle involves the laws of this world in any way, we haven't understood what it is.

Our minds need to change before we can understand

For that matter, the Course seems to assume, in some places, that until some considerable changes have been made in our thinking, we cannot really understand what a miracle is. In Chapter 16, it says, "Why should you worry how the miracle extends to all the Sonship when you do not understand the miracle itself?" (T-16.II.1:6) The idea being expressed, quite clearly, is that we can receive and extend miracles without really understanding what they are; perhaps being able to define a miracle is of lesser importance than receiving them and giving them.

This is after fifteen chapters that have talked an awful lot about miracles! So I don't think we should expect to have a foolproof, rock-solid definition of the word "miracle." Any definition we give is going to seem a little vague, I'm afraid, at least until we have begun to *experience* miracles so that we know them by personal acquaintance. An academic definition simply isn't going to do a lot for us.

Don't fear, though; we *will* give a definition, and by the time we are through, I think it will make some sense.

A miracle cannot be defined in terms of outward changes

Another reason we have trouble pinning down what a miracle is is that a miracle doesn't really *do* anything. It doesn't *change* anything.

A miracle is a correction. It does not create, nor really change at all. It merely looks on devastation, and reminds the mind that what it sees is false. It undoes error, but does not attempt to go beyond perception, nor exceed the function of forgiveness (W-pII.13. 1:1-4).

So a miracle doesn't change anything; it does not create anything new. It does not *do*, it *undoes* error. Our minds are geared to see things that *do something*. We have trouble understanding what a miracle is because we expect it to be like other things we know. We expect it to be like a pill, that works by chemical action. It isn't like that.

The Course contradicts even our traditional understanding of miracles: We think of a miracle as something spectacular and dramatically obvious; the Course says they do not always have observable effects. We think of "impossible" physical healings as being miracles; the Course says that the object of healing is not making the body well. We think of miracles primarily in terms of our bodies and the overturning of physical laws; the Course says that the miracle affects primarily our minds, not our bodies or physical environment. We think of miracles as unusual occurrences; the Course says they are natural and not rare. So, again, our definition will need to take these differences with traditional understanding into account.

Two aspects of the miracle: Receiving miracles and giving them

To help us understand what the Course says about miracles, we need to realize that it is really talking about two entirely different aspects of miracles: miracles that we receive from God, and miracles we give to others. Some of the things the Course talks about as being *prerequisites* for miracles in the second sense (giving them) are actually the *results* of miracles in the first sense (receiving them), which can seem quite confusing. Let me explain a bit more.

First, there are miracles that we *receive*. This aspect of miracles is a personal kind of thing, an interaction between ourselves and the Holy Spirit. Second, there are miracles that we *give*. This aspect of miracles is, in the words of the Course, "genuinely interpersonal." And, in fact, the first aspect of miracles is the prerequisite for the second aspect; we must receive miracles for ourselves before we can give miracles to others. "The miracle that you receive, you give" (T-25.IX.10:1). Lesson 159, "I give the miracles I have received," begins with the words, "No one can give what he has not received" (W-pI.159.1:1).

That can be confusing as you read about what the conditions for miracles are, for instance. As we will discuss in more detail below, the precondition for *giving* a miracle is that you must be, just for an instant at least, in your right mind. That would lead me to think, at first, that right-mindedness is a condition for miracles—in general. But how could that be? How could I *get* to a state of right-mindedness without a miracle? I have often said that attaining the state of right-mindedness or true perception is the goal of the Course; how could the goal of the Course be the *precondition* for miracles? We'd have to be at the end of the curriculum before we ever experienced any miracles, and that certainly isn't the impression we get about miracles from the Course itself.

So, right-mindedness must be the condition for the second aspect: giving, or extending miracles to others. But in order for us to extend or give miracles, we first must receive a miracle ourselves, which is what puts our minds into a right-minded state. (Note that there seems to be a multiplying effect. That is, we may receive a miracle, singular, and give many miracles. Singular or plural, however, the receiving always precedes the giving.) That first aspect—receiving the miracle—must have other, hopefully simpler, conditions.

With that in mind, let's look at some of the things in the Course that are involved with miracles but which are not actually the miracle itself. By talking about the things that surround a miracle, things that come before it, the context of it, and its results, we can *eliminate* some of the things that *are not* a miracle; that will pave the way for us to arrive at a better understanding of the definition.

The preparation for miracles

The Course tells us, in a number of different ways, that miracles need to be prepared for.

Miracles arise from a miraculous state of mind, or a state of miracle-readiness (T-1.I.43:1).

There are certain conditions we must meet in order to receive miracles and to offer them to others. It's easy to confuse that preparation with the miracle itself, so by identifying these conditions, we can set them aside as parts of what a miracle actually is.

Deciding not to wait on time any longer than necessary

The basic decision of the miracle-minded is not to wait on time any longer than is necessary (T-1.V.2:1).

Waiting on time, or expecting the passage of time to somehow resolve the situation or solve the problem we are confronting, is a mind-set that belongs to this world. It means that we are expecting natural laws, over time, to somehow provide the solution. Part of being ready for a miracle, or becoming "miracle-minded," is making the decision *not* to wait on time any more than is necessary, which implies that we have decided not to be bound by time any longer.

To me, this seems to be one of the conditions for my receiving a miracle for myself. I have to stop expecting things to go on as they always have; I have to begin expecting something *different*, something that does not need to take time.

Wanting everyone to be free along with ourselves

Complete restoration of the Sonship is the only goal of the miracle-minded (T-1.VII.3:14).

The impersonal nature of miracle-mindedness... (T-1.III.8:5).

One of the aspects of miracle-mindedness is recognizing that everyone is worthy of miracles. Miracle-mindedness is an "impersonal" state of mind because it does not take differences between persons into account; everyone is included. We see that miracles belong to everyone. We are not simply seeking a miracle for ourselves; we are seeking miracles for everyone. Since arriving at this state of mind is part of being *ready* for miracles, it is obviously not part of the miracle itself.

The Course says many times in different ways that if I am unwilling to share the miracle with my brothers—if I see it as something for myself alone—then I am blocking the miracle from coming to me. So, even in receiving a miracle for myself, there is an interpersonal aspect. I can't expect a miracle, for instance, to give me something in which someone else loses so that I can gain.

Expecting something that exceeds our own abilities

It is much more helpful to remind you that you do not guard your thoughts carefully enough. You may feel that at this point it would take a miracle to enable you to do this, which is perfectly true. You are not used to miracle-minded thinking, but you can be trained to think that way. All miracle workers need that kind of training (T-2.VII.1:7-10).

According to this passage, we are correct to think that for us to guard our thoughts carefully would take a miracle. It tells us that "is perfectly true." But miracle-minded thinking *expects* something that transcends our own abilities, and we need to be trained to think that way, to expect miracles, rather than thinking we are limited to plodding along using just the abilities we now find in ourselves.

Deciding to end the separation, to join our will with God's

The Holy Spirit is the motivation for miracle-mindedness; the decision to heal the separation by letting it go....God Himself keeps your will alive by transmitting it from His Mind to yours as long as there is time. The miracle itself is a reflection of this union of will between Father and Son (T-5.II.1:4,6-7).

Miracle-mindedness involves a "decision to heal the separation by letting it go." It means uniting our will with God's, recognizing that we want what God wants, and He wants what we truly want. Again, that union of our will with God's is not the miracle; "the miracle itself is a *reflection* of this union of will." Miracles will begin to happen for us when our wills—our goals and our purposes in life—have been joined with the Will of God.

Rejoining cause to its effects (our thoughts to our suffering)

Another precondition of miracles is said to be recognizing our thoughts as the cause of our experiences of pain and sickness, rather than projecting the blame for such experiences on things outside of ourselves.

The miracle is possible when cause and consequence are brought together, not kept separate (T-26.VII.14:1).

[Miracles] are the glad effects of taking back the consequence of sickness to its cause. The body is released because the mind acknowledges "this is not done to me, but *I* am doing this." And thus the mind is free to make another choice instead (T-28.II.12:4-6).

What is being discussed here is what I call the *reversal of projection*. Instead of projecting blame onto some external cause, the mind recognizes that its own thoughts are the only cause. In that recognition, it is free to make another choice. And the miracle is not that change of mind, but it is the *effect* of that change of mind. The miracle is what happens when we bring the cause—our thoughts—together with their effects—our experience of suffering, or what we often refer to as our problems. (We are getting close to the definition of a miracle here, but this isn't it yet!)

The next two conditions for miracles are primarily the conditions for giving and extending miracles to others; as you will see, they both more or less assume that we have already received the miracle for ourselves.

Becoming right-minded

The term "right-mindedness" is properly used as the correction for "wrong-mindedness," and applies to the state of mind that induces accurate perception. It is miracle-minded because it heals misperception, and this is indeed a miracle in view of how you perceive yourself (T-3.IV.4:3-4).

I have already said that miracles are expressions of miracle-mindedness, and miracle-mindedness means right-mindedness....It is essential...that the miracle worker be in his right mind, however briefly, or he will be unable to re-establish right-mindedness in someone else (T-2.V.3:1,5).

First of all, let's notice the last part of what we read. There, working a miracle is identified with *re-establishing right-mindedness in someone else.* Therefore, it must take a miracle to establish right-mindedness. But if the condition for being able to do this is that, however briefly, "the miracle worker must be in his right mind," then obviously the miracle worker must have first received a miracle for himself. "I give the miracles I have received" (W-pI.159.Title). Therefore, to say that right-mindedness is a condition for working miracles—which is what I am saying, and what the Course says here—is really just another way of saying that we must receive a miracle before we can give it.

Miracles are not right-mindedness; they are "expressions" of right-mindedness, something that results from or is based upon right-mindedness. To give a miracle we must be in our right mind. Right-mindedness is the effect of the miracle. Therefore, we must receive a miracle that places us in our right mind before we can extend a miracle to someone else, which establishes right-mindedness in that someone else.

Truly accepting the cause of healing

> You have accepted healing's cause, and so it must be you are healed. And being healed, the power to heal must also now be yours. The miracle is not a separate thing that happens suddenly, as an effect without a cause. Nor is it, in itself, a cause. But where its cause is must it be (T-29.II.2:1-5).

The "cause" being referred to here, I believe, could be summed up in the word "Atonement." Atonement is both a *principle* and a *power*. The principle of Atonement is that we are not separate from God, that a split from God never occurred, and therefore we are not separate beings in bodies, but spirit, eternally joined with God. The power of Atonement is the healing activity of the Holy Spirit that ends the apparent effects of that split by showing that the split never happened. When we have accepted Atonement for ourselves, we are in a position to give and receive miracles, but not until then. The Atonement is thus the causative power, and the miracles we receive and offer are its effects.

I think this is very much the same thing as what we saw about right-mindedness. Our accepting the Atonement is not the miracle. The Atonement acts on our minds and gives us a miracle; because of that miracle, we are able to accept the Atonement for ourselves and become right-minded. Our acceptance of the Atonement is the effect of a miracle within our minds, and it is the *cause* of the miracle being extended to others.

In looking at what the Course says prepares us for miracles, I have been trying to eliminate many of the things that we have often confused with miracles. The miracle is not right-mindedness, a state of mind in which we desire healing for everyone and recognize the cause of suffering as being in our own minds and not outside of us. It is not the "normal" changing of things over time; it disregards time. It is not something within the framework of our natural abilities. It is not joining our will with God's Will, nor accepting the Atonement for ourselves. All of these things are parts of miracle-mindedness, and the miracles we offer are the effects of these things. The miracle is *something more than all of these things.*

The context of miracles

By "the context of miracles," I mean the circumstances in which miracles occur, or the birthplace of miracles. Again, the idea of context implies something that *precedes* the miracle and fosters it or encourages it to happen. If something is part of the context of miracles, then that thing is not the miracle, although it is very closely associated with the miracle.

Forgiveness

Forgiveness is very closely linked to the miracle. When I forgive, miracles follow. The Course says:

> Forgiveness is the home of miracles. The eyes of Christ deliver them to all they look upon in mercy and in love. Perception stands corrected in His sight, and what was meant to curse has come to bless. Each lily of forgiveness offers all the world the silent miracle of love (W-pII.13.3:1-4).

"Forgiveness is the *home* of miracles." Forgiveness is where miracles live, where they occur; it is the content they both express and deliver. So forgiveness is *not* the same as a miracle, although the two are very closely associated. They are like two sides of a single coin. Forgiveness has to do with the undoing aspect; it overlooks the appearance of sin. It removes the obstacles. "Every miracle is but the end of an illusion" (T-19.IV(A).6:8). I must be willing to forgive, to see past the appearance of sin. Forgiveness is the willingness to have the miracle shift me from my grievance to love.

When forgiveness occurs, the miracle takes the place of what forgiveness has overlooked. Love, which had been blocked by unforgiveness, can flow again.

> And I invite the solution to come to me through my forgiveness of the grievance, and my welcome of the miracle that takes its place (W-pI.rII.90.1:6).

The miracle, then, is something that takes the place of a grievance when I forgive that grievance and I welcome the miracle. In experience, I think, these two aspects are nearly indistinguishable. There is no time lag; the instant I forgive, the miracle rushes in to replace my grievance, bringing with it a new perception, a different vision that sees truth rather than illusion:

> The miracle forgives because it stands for what is past forgiveness and is true (T-27.VI.6:2).

This seems to be almost identifying the miracle with forgiveness: "The miracle forgives." Yet in the second part of the sentence, we can see that the miracle is more than just forgiveness: "It stands for what is past forgiveness and is true." The miracle reflects or represents the truth; it brings us a vision of something that has always been true, something that has been hidden from us by our grievances. The miracle shows us innocence and sinlessness.

Christ's vision

Forgiveness brings miracles; miracles are an experience of Christ's vision. Vision has two senses, one that which is seen, and two, the act or ability of seeing:

> And they will look upon the vision of the Son of God, remembering who he is they sing of. What is a miracle but this remembering? (T-21.I.10:3-4).

> Christ's vision is the miracle in which all miracles are born. It is their source, remaining with each miracle you give, and yet remaining yours (W-pI.159.4:1-2).

The miracle that Christ gives to us brings us His vision; what that vision shows us is the Christ, the Son of God. To paraphrase the above, "What is a miracle but remembering the vision of the Son of God?" The miracle is a remembering. The reality of God's Son which we see is always there; vision only affects our *awareness* of that reality. Thus, Christ's vision is both the *source* and *content* of miracles. It is their source in the sense that this ability to perceive reality, given us by God, is what produces the experience of a miracle. It is the content of each miracle we share ("each miracle you give"), for each time we remember and see Christ in one another, that *is* the miracle. Therefore, Christ's vision can be called "the miracle in which all miracles are born." It is the father of miracles. Every miracle is, in some sense, a vision of Christ.

Both forgiveness and miracles have to do with releasing sin. Forgiveness says I am willing to overlook sin. The miracle then completes this process by wiping away the perception of sin and the punishing effects that come from sin, and showing us something else in its place: the vision of the Son of God.

The holy instant

Another thing the Course talks about a lot is the holy instant. And once again, because the holy instant is the moment in which we receive and offer miracles, it is easy to confuse the two. But they aren't quite the same. Just as forgiveness is called the home of miracles, the Course says, "The holy instant is the miracle's abiding place" (T-27.V.3:1). "Home" and "abiding place" are synonymous, so basically the holy instant bears the same relationship to the miracle that forgiveness does.

In a nutshell, I see it like this: The holy instant is the instant in which I receive a miracle, and from that state of mind, miracles extend to others. We can see this in two passages:

> There is one thing that you have never done; you have not utterly forgotten the body. It has perhaps faded at times from your sight, but it has not yet completely disappeared. You are not asked to let this happen for more than an instant, yet it is in this instant that the miracle of Atonement happens (T-18.VII.2:1-3).

So here we see that the miracle of Atonement *happens* in the holy instant—that is the first aspect of the miracle, in which we receive the Atonement for ourselves. Second, miracles extend from the holy instant:

> Seek and *find* His message in the holy instant, where all illusions are forgiven. From there the miracle extends to bless everyone and to resolve all problems, be they perceived as great or small, possible or impossible (T-16.VII.11:1-2).

In the holy instant, we experience the miracle, in which all illusions are forgiven. And *from* the holy instant, the miracle extends to everyone, which is the second aspect of miracles. In that sense, as we have already seen, the holy instant is the abiding place or home of miracles:

> The holy instant is the miracle's abiding place. From there, each one is born into this world as witness to a state of mind that has transcended conflict, and has reached to peace (T-27.V.3:1-2).

11

So, in looking at the holy instant as the context in which miracles occur, we can see that a holy instant is an instant in which we receive a miracle, and from that instant miracles extend to others. The term "holy instant" refers, to be specific, to an interval of time, and also to the experience within that interval. And what is experienced in the holy instant is the miracle. Just as with forgiveness, there is a part of miracles which is nearly identical with the holy instant, and another part—the extension part, the vision of Christ part—which goes beyond it.

The source of miracles

We'll be very brief here. The Source of miracles is Jesus, or the Holy Spirit. (In different parts of the Text, the miracle is attributed both to the Holy Spirit and to Jesus.[1]) We do not do them. They aren't anything we do. This is especially emphasized concerning the extension aspect of miracles. The Course is very, very clear about this:

> Concern yourself not with the extension of holiness, for the nature of miracles you do not understand. Nor do you do them. It is their extension, far beyond the limits you perceive, that demonstrates you do not do them (T-16.II.1:3-5).

> The Holy Spirit is the mechanism of miracles (T-1.I.38:1).

> I have said that the Holy Spirit is the motivation for miracles (T-6.V(A).3:1).

In offering or extending miracles, our cooperation is necessary. But the motivation for miracles, choosing the specific recipients to whom we offer them, and the mechanism by which they happen, do not come from us. We offer miracles under the direction of Jesus, and through the Holy Spirit.

> Offer Christ's gift to everyone and everywhere, for miracles, offered the Son of God through the Holy Spirit, attune you to reality. The Holy Spirit knows your part in the redemption, and who are seeking you and where to find them (T-13.VIII.7:2-3).

---

[1]Jesus, in *A Course in Miracles*, is said to be "the manifestation of the Holy Spirit" (C-6.1:1). Therefore, it makes perfect sense to say that a miracle is done by Jesus, or that a miracle is done by the Holy Spirit. Both are true, since one way the Holy Spirit acts is through Jesus.

We need to be ready to offer miracles to everyone, everywhere, but the specific persons to whom we offer miracles—the ones who are seeking us—only the Holy Spirit knows, and will show to us. In the first quote that follows you can see that both Jesus and the Holy Spirit are involved in "arranging" our miracle-giving:

> In time, you have been told to offer miracles as I direct, and let the Holy Spirit bring to you those who are seeking you (T-15.V.10:7).

> The power to work miracles belongs to you. I will provide the opportunities to do them, but you must be ready and willing (T-1.III.1:7-8).

The interpersonal nature of miracles

Several times in the beginning of the Text the miracle is contrasted with revelation. Revelation is a direct experience of God, something that happens between you and God, while a miracle, by contrast, is interpersonal, involving another person with you. Revelation is not a miracle.

Miracles are said to be more valuable to us now than revelation:

> Revelation is intensely personal and cannot be meaningfully translated. That is why any attempt to describe it in words is impossible. Revelation induces only experience. Miracles, on the other hand, induce action. They are more useful now because of their interpersonal nature (T-1.II.2:1-5).

What I want to establish here, primarily, is that revelation and miracles are different, and that miracles (in their extension aspect) are interpersonal, involving you *and someone else.*

That aspect of miracles—the aspect of extension, involving another person—is simply inescapable in discussing miracles in the Course. You cannot really understand all that is said about miracles unless you include extension, and it is their extension that most clearly demonstrates that they are something from beyond this world, rather than something we are doing ourselves. We already quoted this passage, but I'll quote it again:

> Concern yourself not with the extension of holiness, for the nature of miracles you do not understand. Nor do you do them. It is their extension, far beyond the limits you perceive, that demonstrates you do not do them (T-16.II.1:3-5).

The Answer Is a Miracle

The results of miracles

We're getting near the end here! We've seen that there are certain ways that we need to *prepare* ourselves for miracles. We've seen that miracles occur in the *context* of forgiveness and the holy instant, in which we receive the miracle for ourselves. Then, Jesus directs us about extending them, and the Holy Spirit brings those to us who are to receive them, and He empowers them, He actually *does* the extending. He through us, and we through Him.

There are results when we receive a miracle, and other results when we give or extend one.

The results of receiving a miracle: perception shifts

When we receive the miracle, we are told, it shifts our perception. As Jesus put it in the line we quoted earlier:

A miracle is a correction introduced into false thinking by me [Jesus]. It acts as a catalyst, breaking up erroneous perception and reorganizing it properly (T-1.I.37:1-2).

I think it is important here to notice that the very common definition given to a miracle by many Course students is not strictly correct. Many students define a miracle as "a shift in perception." There is definitely a shift in perception going on here, false perception is being broken up and reorganized. But that is the *result* of the miracle and not, strictly speaking, the miracle itself. There are a number of passages in the Course in which a miracle is connected to a shift in perception, and in every case the relationship is not one of identity, but one of cause and effect. If it were an identity it would mean that a miracle *is* a shift in perception. If the relationship is one of cause and effect, then a miracle *causes* a shift in perception. Here are several of those passages, in which I have placed emphasis on the cause and effect relationship:

Miracles *rearrange* perception and place all levels in true perspective (T-1.I.23.1).

...the miracle *entails a sudden shift* from horizontal to vertical perception (T-1.II.6:3).

The level-adjustment power of the miracle *induces* the right perception for healing (T-2.V(A).15:1).

...the *shift in the perception* of time that *the miracle introduces* (T-5.II.1:3).

A miracle inverts perception which was upside down before, and thus it ends the strange distortions that were manifest (W-pII.13.2:3).

Father, I wake today with *miracles correcting my perception* of all things (W-pII.346.1:1).

I think that if we confuse the miracle with the shift in perception that the miracle produces, then we may be inclined to think that it's a miracle whenever we change our minds. Calling a miracle a shift in perception makes it too easy to think that a miracle is something *we do*. And it isn't; it is something the Holy Spirit or Jesus does. That something then *introduces, entails,* or *induces* a shift in our perception. Our shift in perception is the result of a divine action.

The results of extending a miracle: it returns; visible effects

Finally, there are certain results from the extension of miracles. First of all, the miracle you extend returns to you. What you give, you receive. This is a pattern that should become familiar as you study the Text: We receive something, we choose to share that something, and in sharing it, it returns to us, strengthened and reinforced. It is by giving that we *recognize* that we have received; it is by allowing the Holy Spirit to work through us that we know He is in us.

Another result of miracles *may be* actual changes in external circumstances. While miracles do not always have observable results, they often do. "Miracles are expressions of love, but they may not always have observable effects" (T-1.I.35:1). Bodies may be healed. Relationships may be transformed. Things that seem impossible may happen. All sorts of things may happen—but not always. These things are not the miracle, but they are among the results of a miracle.

The definition of a miracle

We are almost ready now to define a miracle. We've already seen certain aspects of it; we just need to bring them together. We've eliminated a lot of things! So what is left?

Let's go back to the very first quotation we used in Chapter One:

A miracle is a correction introduced into false thinking by me [Jesus] (T-1.I.37:1).

The key element of this statement and, to me, the defining characteristic of a miracle, is that the miracle is something Jesus (or the Holy Spirit) does. A miracle is not something we do, but something that is done *to us* or *through us* by the Holy Spirit. It is a divine action, a way in which God, through the Holy Spirit and through Jesus, adjusts our false thinking. Since it is the activity of the Holy Spirit, I cannot bring about a miracle by any kind of effort or activity; indeed, my effort and activity just gets in the way. All I can do is to open myself to receive, and to ask. That said, let me present now a fuller definition of a miracle.

The remainder of this chapter, beginning with the next paragraph, was written by Robert; it encapsulates his study of all the places in the Course where the words "a miracle is..." or "miracles are..." occur. My contribution to this chapter has been nothing more than a long preface to this outstanding summary. Consider now with Robert the situation in which we seem to find ourselves in this world. First, Robert looks at our *apparent* predicament, and what, in the light of that picture, we traditionally think of as a miracle. Then, he looks at our *actual* situation, and what, in the light of that picture, a miracle really is. Finally, he summarizes all of this into a succinct definition of the word "miracle." We will be expanding on this material throughout the next several chapters, in the form of eleven points which look at our apparent predicament, along with the Course's answer to each of those eleven points, found in its teaching about miracles.

Our apparent predicament

We seem to be imprisoned by forces beyond our control, by the world and its laws, and by the past. This leaves us hemmed in by countless problems, difficulties, griefs and sicknesses, some of which seem quite large and impossible to solve. We must, therefore, devote all our power and wisdom to solving these problems. By working skillfully within the laws that imprison us, we may be able to escape from some of our problems, yet this still is a slow, precarious process.

The traditional miracle

Only a miracle could deliver us. A miracle is a divine healing of earthly sicknesses, problems and difficulties, in which the Spirit enters and supersedes normal earthly laws, and brings instantaneous healing in ways considered impossible. Yet miracles are so rare we cannot count on them. To receive them we must wait on divine whim to arbitrarily blow our way. We know, however, that miracles are given to God's elect, so perhaps we can earn our way into that special category. Even then there are some problems that the miracle itself probably cannot solve. And even if a miracle comes to heal our crisis situation, will we not still be left with our basic condition of being an unhappy person at the mercy of an imprisoning world?

Our actual situation

We are not actually imprisoned by the world, its laws, its past and its unending barrage of external problems. We are imprisoned only by our mind's belief in the *reality* of the world, only by our mind's *perception* of the world. In truth all that seems to imprison and limit us is unreal. We are thus already free of every possible confinement. We are unlimited spirit in the Mind of God. Therefore, total and instantaneous deliverance is offered us in every moment, waiting only for our acceptance of it.

The ACIM miracle

Miracles are instances of total, unconditional, instantaneous and free deliverance from the imprisoning problems, sicknesses and suffering of this world. They heal all problems with equal ease, regardless of their differences in kind, size or gravity. Rather than working within the laws that imprison us, they have complete power over the laws of time and space. For their purpose is to release us from the "reality" of those laws, to show us *we* are not bound by them, that we are cause and the world is illusory effect.

The miracle is the activity of the Holy Spirit, which enters our minds in a holy instant when normal thought and perception is momentarily suspended, when we have been willing to bring cause (our thinking) and effect (our pain) together. The miracle then shifts our minds from false perception to true perception, from belief in this world's reality to realization of true reality, from fear to love, from bondage to freedom. It thus releases our minds from the painful emotional effects of false perception (based on belief in sin), including fear, guilt, anger and anxiety. It frees us as well from the *physical* effects of our supposed sins, proving that those effects are not real because they can change, and proving that their cause (sin) is not real because it has no effects. The miracle frees us from the prison of the past and thus releases the future. It collapses time, freeing us from certain intervals of time (intervals as long as thousands of years). It frees us from having to free ourselves. For it is the Holy Spirit, not us, Who does miracles and Who understands how they work. The miracle frees us instantaneously, for it does not respect time and its law of gradual change. It frees us from having to earn our deliverance, for the miracle is natural. It is our right. Thus it is completely in our hands when we choose to claim the miracle. We are freed of having to wait for it, for it is always there, waiting on *us*.

We are called to be miracle workers, to miraculously release *others* from their imprisonment, but first we must accept miracle-mindedness for ourselves.

The miracles we accept into our own mind will naturally and automatically extend through us. Even though this extension will often involve our physical action, it should ideally be involuntary. When, how and to whom we give miracles should be directed by the Holy Spirit. In giving a miracle, our right-mindedness will shine into the mind of the miracle receiver, awakening that mind to the same right-minded state, freeing it from false perception and all effects (including physical effects) of false perception. By giving the miracle, we will receive it. In the effects they produce in others and in the gratitude which others return to us, miracles bear witness to the state of holiness in us from which they came. They thus strengthen that state in us, and also teach us that giving and receiving are the same.

All miracles are the same. They are the one solution to every problem, the one answer to every call for help. Each one carries all of God's power, and each one is for everyone. The miracle that we receive for ourselves we naturally give to another. The miracle we give to another we do not lose, but receive for ourselves. This same miracle may affect people across the world. It will also affect the entire Sonship, for it is given to everyone equally. The miracle thus transcends this world's laws by benefiting as one both giver and receiver, immediate receiver and distant receiver, and literally everyone and everything.

A short definition of "miracle"

A miracle is the activity of the Holy Spirit which shifts our perception from false to true and thereby grants us unconditional, instantaneous and free deliverance from the imprisoning (yet illusory) problems of this world. We accept miracles (into our own minds), extend them (to others) and so recognize that we have received them.

-2-
Miracles Free Us from the Laws of This World

by Robert

B eginning here and for the next several chapters we will be exploring eleven points of contrast between the miracle and our conventional notions of reality. This chapter will cover the first of those points.

1. We seem to be imprisoned by the physical world and its laws. The world seems to be cause and we its effect.

This, of course, is our conventional view. We appear to be captives of the laws of this world. Lesson 76 in the Workbook asks us to mentally review the different laws we believe we must obey. To help us do so, in Paragraph 8 it mentions three kinds of laws:

> **1. Bodily laws:** "For example, the 'laws' of nutrition, of immunization, of medication, and of the body's protection in innumerable ways."

> **2. Relationship laws:** "You believe in the 'laws' of friendship, of 'good' relationships and reciprocity."

> **3. Religious laws:** "Perhaps you even think that there are laws which set forth what is God's and what is yours."

What is the essence of the idea of "law"? A law, in our normal thinking, is something that you must obey or suffer the consequences. Laws by their very nature are imprisoning because they demand obedience. But they become especially imprisoning when not obeyed. You may think that laws against stealing, for example, hamper your freedom (in this case, your freedom to take things), but this hampering gets much worse if you actually break those laws and land behind bars.

We can immediately see this essential quality with all three kinds of laws above. If we do not obey the laws of nutrition what happens? We become malnourished. If we do not get immunized, we are vulnerable to certain diseases. If we do not take our medicine, we stay sick. We either obey the law or suffer the consequences.

Going on to the second class of laws, if we do not obey the laws of friendship, people cease to act friendly toward us. If we do not obey the law of reciprocity—if we do not reciprocate—people soon stop giving to us. These relationship laws are unwritten, but no less powerful because of it. When you break some law of social etiquette or some cultural code, people know it, and respond accordingly.

The same pattern holds true with religious laws. According to most religions, if we do not obey the laws of that religion, dire consequences will follow. In one form or another, we fall out of God's graces. The gulf between "what is God's and what is yours" widens. We feel His frown overshadowing us, we fear some earthly calamity befalling us, and we know that the full punishment awaits us in the life beyond.

Once we start reflecting on all the laws we are obeying, and all the corresponding threats we live under, we get a sense of just how thoroughly imprisoned we feel. We run around all day long obeying an endless list of laws, for our health and safety, for our entertainment and enjoyment, for our love and companionship, for our sense of being right with God. Nothing is free. Everything comes with a price, the price of our obedience.

Clearly, we are not the ones in charge here. That at least is our experience, and that is the message we get from birth onward. The world we live in functions like a giant penal colony, and we, as its prisoners, have only a tiny range in which to exercise our freedom. According to our experience, the world is cause and we are effect.

1A. The miracle frees us from the world and its laws, revealing the mind as cause and the world as effect and as unreal.

Based on how imprisoned we feel, what would it be like to be free of the laws of this world? This, of course, is something we all have fantasized about at one time or another. What if we could have a disease healed instantaneously? What if our bodies were not so vulnerable to the weather, or to the ravages of time? What if we didn't have to work so hard at pleasing people all the time—or at pleasing God, for that matter?

This is one purpose of the miracle. It overturns the laws of this world, especially the laws of physical disease. Over and over the Course states or implies that miracles heal sick bodies. I realize that in the eyes of many Course students a miracle has nothing to do with such mundane things. Yet the Course simply contains too many references to a miracle overturning the laws of this world to allow us to maintain such a position. Here are a couple:

> Since the miracle aims at restoring the awareness of reality, it would not be useful if it were bound by laws [in this case, the law of size] that govern the error it aims to correct (T-1.III.9:4).

> The Holy Spirit is invisible, but you can see the results of His Presence, and through them you will learn that He is there. What He enables you to do is clearly not of this world, for miracles violate every law of reality as this world judges it. Every law of time and space, of magnitude and mass is transcended, for what the Holy Spirit enables you to do is clearly beyond all of them (T-12.VII.3:1-3).

This second passage is especially clear. It tells us that miracles produce visible results, results you can see. These results come from the fact that miracles violate *every* law of visible "reality." This includes the laws of time, space, magnitude and mass. Based on this, when miracles occur we should expect to see physical masses instantaneously altered.

Yet doesn't the act of changing physical appearances imply that those appearances are real? The Course clearly teaches that the world is an illusion. Why, then, would the Holy Spirit go around changing it with miracles? Doesn't dignifying the world with an answer, well, dignify it, give it a certain amount of importance and reality? This argument sounds reasonable enough, yet the Course's perspective is quite different, as we will see in the following section.

Miracles show that appearances are unreal because they can so easily be changed.

The Course turns the above line of reasoning on its head. By changing the realm of form, it says, miracles prove that form is *unreal*. In one passage, the Course claims that reality is changeless and then goes on to say:

> The miracle is means to demonstrate that all appearances can change because they *are* appearances, and cannot have the changelessness reality entails. The miracle attests salvation from appearances by showing they can change. Your brother has a changelessness in him beyond appearance and deception, both....The miracle is proof he is not bound by loss or suffering in any form, because it can so easily

be changed. This demonstrates that it was never real, and could not stem from his reality. For that is changeless, and has no effects that anything in Heaven or on earth could ever alter. But appearances are shown to be unreal *because* they change (T-30.VIII.2:1-3,6-9).

This paragraph says the same thing in many different ways. By changing physical appearances, the miracle proves that they are not real, for what is real cannot change. This means that miracles deliver us from the tyranny of form in *two* distinct ways. First, the miracle frees us from a particular form; a particular disease, for instance. Second, by changing this form, the miracle proves that it was never real in the first place. So in the very act of unbinding us the miracle proves we cannot be bound, for it reveals that the things that bind us are unreal.

Miracles show that the laws of this world are powerless

How foolish and insane it is to think a miracle is bound by laws that it came solely to undo! The laws of sin have different witnesses with different strengths. And they attest to different sufferings. Yet to the One Who sends forth miracles to bless the world, a tiny stab of pain, a little worldly pleasure, and the throes of death itself are but a single sound; a call for healing, and a plaintive cry for help within a world of misery. It is their sameness that the miracle attests. It is their sameness that it proves. The laws that call them different are dissolved, and shown as powerless. The purpose of a miracle is to accomplish this (T-27.VI.6:3-10).

This passage opens by making the exact same point as a passage we read earlier, which said "it would not be useful if [the miracle] were bound by laws that govern the error it aims to correct" (T-1.III.9:4). The miracle has come to undo the world's laws. How, then, could it be bound by them? The very "purpose of a miracle" is to show the world's laws to be powerless. In the above passage, a miracle does this by healing with total indiscriminateness. It heals "a tiny stab of pain, a little worldly pleasure, and the throes of death itself" without any regard for their apparent differences. By treating them exactly the same, "the laws that call them different are…shown as powerless."

The laws that seem to bind us are powerless. That is what miracles are here to show us. They are here to demonstrate that we are free of the tyranny of this world, free because the world can be changed, and free because the world is unreal.

Miracles show that you are cause and the world is effect

Earlier we saw that we experience ourselves as effects, the world being our apparent cause. We seem to have a certain amount of freedom, but it is freedom in *response* to the world's events, freedom *within* parameters it sets up. This is so fundamental to our experience here that we hardly think about it. Yet imagine how it would feel if this were suddenly reversed. Imagine suddenly experiencing yourself as the cause and the world as your effect, so that you were no longer a slave to hundreds of oppressive laws, but were free to express your highest and most joyous impulses freely and without impediment. According to the Course, the miracle is here to show you that this is already the case, and always has been.

> This world is full of miracles. They stand in shining silence next to every dream of pain and suffering, of sin and guilt. They are the dream's alternative, the choice to be the dreamer, rather than deny the active role in making up the dream. They are the glad effects of taking back the consequence of sickness to its cause. The body is released because the mind acknowledges "this is not done to me, but *I* am doing this" (T-28.II.12:1-5).

Each of our lives contains many dreams of "pain and suffering, of sin and guilt." We may have a painful marriage, an unrewarding job, an unhealed relationship with our father or mother, a lack of finances, a chronic disease. Next to each one of these painful dreams stands a miracle "in shining silence," patiently waiting to set us free. We accept this miracle by acknowledging our role as the dreamer. We had an "active role in making up" this painful condition. We dreamt it. It is not being done to us. We are doing it.

When we fully acknowledge this, the miracle switches from standing there in silence to leaping into action. It releases our body, heals our marriage, supplies our lack. In doing so it visibly demonstrates the principle that brought it to us. Being of the mind, the miracle proves that the mind is cause and the world is mere effect.

By removing effects, miracles prove that their cause (sin) is unreal

The Course suggests that somewhere in our minds we know that the painful conditions in our lives were caused by us. In this place we see those outer difficulties as the direct effect of our inner sinfulness. We see them as the proof that we are miserable sinners. The Course says that "the ego sees [the connection between the mind and outer difficulty] as proof of sin" (T-19.IV(B).12:2). All of us can probably remember interpreting things this way at one time or another. Something "bad" happens to us and we wonder aloud, "What did I do to deserve this?" Or we think we know what we did. We secretly suspect that this calamity is punishment for some specific "sin" of our past.

So, in the psychology of the ego, outer difficulties are the proof that there exists in us a corresponding cause, a sin that merits this chastisement. What, then, if a miracle comes and removes this outer difficulty? Using the same reasoning we must conclude that the inner cause, our sin, does not exist. Causes by nature produce effects. Sins by nature call for punishments. If, therefore, the punishing effect is gone, then its cause must be nonexistent as well.

> The miracle returns the cause of fear to you who made it [it shows that you caused the outer effects that made you afraid]. But it also shows that, having no effects, it [the sin in you that caused your painful effects] is not cause, because the function of causation is to have effects. And where effects are gone, there is no cause (T-28.II.11:1-3).

Thoughts for application

Let's try to put the above four sections into personal application. Try thinking of some particular problem in your life, something that seems to be binding you in some way. Holding this problem in mind, repeat to yourself the following four ideas. It helps if you do this slowly, training your full awareness on the words you are repeating.

> *I am not bound by this problem. The miracle can easily change it and show me that it is not real.* (based on T-30.VIII.1-2)

> *A miracle can show me that the laws that bind me are powerless.* (based on T-27.VI.6:3-10)

> *I can be released because this is not done to me, but I am doing this.* (based on T-28.II.9,12)

> *The miracle can remove these effects and so show me that their cause, my sin, is unreal.* (based on T-28.II.11:1-3)

Conclusion

We have seen in this chapter that miracles do indeed have an effect on the world of form. Yet, perhaps surprisingly, their purpose in having this effect is not to provide us with pleasant, enjoyable forms. In fact, one of the things they are designed to heal us of is "a little worldly pleasure" (T-27.VI.6:6). Their healing of the world of form is really designed to send our minds a very deep message. This message is that form is unreal, that the laws of form are powerless, that the mind is cause and not effect, and that sin is unreal. Thus, even while miracles are shifting forms around, their purpose is psychological. They are meant to free the mind from its belief in the tyranny of form.

-3-
The Past; the Multitude of Problems

by Allen

2. We seem to be imprisoned by the past.

A ccording to Robert's extended definition, a miracle is the response of the Holy Spirit to our mistakes, by which we are given total, unconditional, instantaneous and free deliverance from the imprisonment of this world. We'll begin our look at the past, therefore, by considering some of the ways the past seems to imprison us.

We see ourselves as forever the result (or effect) of things that were done to us.

One major example concerns our parents. We think our personality and our abilities have been shaped and limited by our parents and the way they raised us.

We also believe that we are limited and bound by things we did not have in the past, such as a happy family life or enough money. Perhaps we grew up in a crowded, dirty city and never enjoyed the countryside. Perhaps we grew up in a rural area and were deprived of the cultural richness of the city. We think this has fixed effects in our lives.

We may have had terrible relationships in the past. Someone may have mistreated us or betrayed us, so that we feel irretrievably scarred by the experience. We may feel these wounds are impossible to overcome.

There are so many ways we can feel that the past has somehow deprived us of something essential or valuable, and that as a result, our present and our future are imprisoned by these unfair limitations.

We seem to be imprisoned by things that we did.

It isn't only what other people or events of the past did to us that seem to limit us. We also see ourselves as the effect of what we, ourselves, have done. Probably the single biggest way in which we see ourselves imprisoned by our past actions is our guilt about past wrongs that we have done to others: guilt over deliberate attacks we have made; unintentional omissions; and even so-called sins of ignorance or accident, where we hurt someone without meaning to do so. Somehow, we feel that our past sins have marked us forever and shown us to be imperfect fools at best, or twisted and depraved souls at worst. Somewhere, God has it all on videotape, and some time after death you are going to sit in a tribunal which will pass judgment on all the terrible and foolish things you have done. You are imprisoned by your sins, forever defined and limited by the things you have done.

We believe we are doomed to repeat the past, particularly failures.
There is what I call, the "I have never..." syndrome. According to this false mental "law," you can never do anything more than what you have done in the past. "I've never had a successful relationship" therefore means you can never have one. "I've never been able to lose weight" means you never will. "I've never been able to meditate" means that you can never learn to meditate. We think our past defines us and limits us.

Just because you have never done it before does not mean you cannot do it now. Just because you have never had a holy instant does not mean that you never will. Just because you have never experienced miraculous healing of your body does not mean that it cannot happen. Just because you have never completely forgiven your father, or mother, or whoever it might be, does not mean that forgiveness is impossible for you. The past does not bind you; you are entitled to miracles.

We get trapped in thinking that our past defines us. But it isn't the past that traps us; it is our *thinking* that has trapped us. We are not defined by what others did to us. We are not defined by things we have done. We are not defined by our past experiences and limitations. This is what a miracle tells us.

2A. The miracle frees us from the past.

Miracles are both beginnings and endings, and so they alter the temporal order. They are always affirmations of rebirth, which seem to go back but really go forward. They undo the past in the present, and thus release the future (T-1.I.13:1-3).

The miracle is a beginning and an ending. It ends something from the past, and it heralds a future different from the past. The activity of the Holy Spirit enters into our minds and breaks up erroneous perception—that's the ending. It then reorganizes perception properly—that is the new beginning.

A miracle *undoes the past* in the present. That is, perhaps, the key, because all of our beliefs about ways in which the past imprisons us are built on one

28

single idea: *the past cannot be changed.* But a miracle undoes the past. To us, the past cannot be undone. "What's done is done" means undoing is impossible. And within the laws of time and space in which we normally operate, that is true. But a miracle is not restricted to those laws. A miracle operates by different laws, the laws of Heaven, where time does not even exist.

When something is very, very old, we call it *ancient.* And if something is ancient, that means it has been around for a long, long time. The longer it has been around, the more real it seems, the more lasting and unchangeable. Yet in a miracle, an ancient hatred can become a present love (T-26.IX.6:1). How can that happen unless the past is undone? A miracle literally rewrites the past. It breaks up erroneous perception, so that we see the past in an entirely different light, a light that justifies love instead of justifying hatred.

Let's look at a section in the Text that really covers this matter of the miracle and the past quite thoroughly. If you wish to read the entire context, read T-28.I, "The Present Memory." It tells us here that the miracle really doesn't "do" anything; it *undoes.* It takes away the past, which has been kept alive in our minds only by our memories. "The miracle but shows the past is gone, and what has truly gone has no effects" (T-28.I.1:8).

A miracle breaks up erroneous perceptions. And *memory* is just the past tense of perception: "Remembering is as selective as perception, being its past tense" (T-28.I.2:5). So therefore, a miracle can break up erroneous memories. The Holy Spirit reaches into your mind and dissolves or disintegrates your memories, your perceptions of the past, and then He reorganizes them. The section continues, telling us that remembering "is perception of the past as if it were occurring now" (T-28.I.2:6), but God can use it to heal instead of hurt.

> The Holy Spirit can indeed make use of memory, for God Himself is there. Yet this is not a memory of past events, but only of a present state (T-28.I.4:1-2).

So in reorganizing our memories, the Holy Spirit not only changes our perceptions of the past, He introduces *memory of a present state.* He reminds us of the eternal and changeless, of what is always true. He shows us present innocence. "The miracle reminds you of a Cause forever present, perfectly untouched by time and interference" (T-28.I.9:4).

The Course calls our use of the past, "as if the past had caused the present," a "strange use of it" (T-28.I.6:4). Isn't that a nearly universal belief—to think that the past caused the present? Yet to think that is to be imprisoned by the past, so we must all be so imprisoned. It is from this kind of temporal imprisonment that the miracle frees us:

The miracle comes quietly into the mind that stops an instant and is still. It reaches gently from that quiet time, and from the mind it healed in quiet then, to other minds to share its quietness. And they will join in doing nothing to prevent its radiant extension back into the Mind Which caused all minds to be. Born out of sharing, there can be no pause in time to cause the miracle delay in hastening to all unquiet minds, and bringing them an instant's stillness, when the memory of God returns to them. Their own remembering is quiet now, and what has come to take its place will not be wholly unremembered afterwards (T-28.I.11:1-5).

So, then, we can see so clearly here that a miracle is a total, unconditional, instantaneous and free deliverance from the imprisonment of the past: the belief that the past causes the present is broken up by the Holy Spirit, and the memory of an eternal, present Cause is reintroduced into our minds, liberating us from all effects of the past. That miracle then extends from our minds to all unquiet minds, bringing to them as well the memory of God.

Thoughts for application

Think of a situation from your past, something you have thought of as unchangeable. Perhaps it was something done to you, or something you did, or something you haven't been able to do in the past that seems to limit you now. Hold that problem from the past in your mind, and then apply these thoughts to it:

Miracles undo the past in the present, and thus release the future. A miracle can undo this past situation for me, and release me to a new future.

The miracle can show me that the past as I remember it is gone, and has no present effects. What I remember never was.

Memory is just how I see the past, which is selective. Memory can be used to heal as well as to hurt. I give my memories now to the Holy Spirit, asking Him to shift them, to use them to heal.

I do not want my memories of hate; their cause is gone. I want the present memory of an eternal, changeless Cause.

I am not the effect of my past; I am forever the effect of God.

3. We seem to be imprisoned by the "many-ness" of our problems.

We also seem imprisoned by the sheer *number* of problems that we have. Even in the context of one relationship, there are scores of problems: problems with habits we don't like in one another, with communication, about finances, about sex, about differences in moral judgment, about where to live, about simplicity versus luxury, about work versus recreation, about raising children, and so on.

And that's just within a single relationship. We have dozens of relationships, each with whole complexes of problems. We have problems with career, problems with health, problems with the government, problems with our cars, problems with household appliances, problems with insect and rodent pests in the home, problems with plant lice, problems with our weight, problems with our computers or lack of computers. We have bad hair days. We have hormones or no hormones. We have problems with aging, problems with preservatives in our food and people and things that don't do their job properly. We have traffic problems. We have problems keeping our house clean, problems organizing things, problems with forgetting things, problems with the weather.

We haven't really touched on our spiritual problems, either. Consider our problems trying to follow the Course. We have problems meditating. We have problems getting to bed early to have time for our practice in the morning. We have problems understanding the Text. We have problems forgiving certain people. We have a problem understanding miracles, with just being happy, with letting go of grievances, or letting go of planning, or letting go of the belief that defenses are necessary. We can't seem to hear the Holy Spirit. The list goes on and on. We are overwhelmed by the number of problems.

Every problem requires a different solution.

What is so draining, frustrating all our efforts at simple survival, is that every problem requires a different, specific solution.

> The world seems to present you with a vast number of problems, each requiring a different answer. This perception places you in a position in which your problem-solving must be inadequate, and failure is inevitable.

> No one could solve all the problems the world appears to hold. They seem to be on so many levels, in such varying forms and with such varied content, that they confront you with an impossible situation. Dismay and depression are inevitable as you regard them.

Some spring up unexpectedly, just as you think you have resolved the previous ones. Others remain unsolved under a cloud of denial, and rise to haunt you from time to time, only to be hidden again but still unsolved (W-pI.79.4:2-5:5).

"Dismay and depression." That describes how we often feel in the face of all our problems. No matter how hard we try we are confronted with an impossible situation, because every problem requires a different answer. Failure is inevitable! How depressing!

We don't have time to solve them all.

Furthermore, paying attention to one problem draws our attention away from all the others. Take time to do your quiet time and suddenly your exercise program is suffering, or you end up being late to work again. Concentrate on that exercise and you find you have spent too much money on running shoes. Focus on work, and your relationship suffers. The whole thing can drive you crazy—and probably has!

A long series of different problems seems to confront you, and as one is settled the next one and the next arise. There seems to be no end to them. There is no time in which you feel completely free of problems and at peace (W-pI.79.3:3-5).

That's how it seems to us, isn't it? There is simply no time in which you feel completely free of problems and at peace!

What has all this got to do with miracles? Well, miracles free us from the seeming laws of this world. They free us from everything that appears to imprison us. And we certainly seem to be imprisoned by the multitude of our problems.

3A. All miracles are the same and all problems are the same. They are the only solution for the only problem.

The first principle of miracles given in the Course is:

There is no order of difficulty in miracles. One is not "harder" or "bigger" than another. They are all the same. All expressions of love are maximal (T-1.I.1:1-4).

If, as this passage says, all miracles are the same, then it must mean that all problems are also the same. We think we have big problems and little problems, but if the same miracle can solve all problems, then all the problems must be the same also. One size fits all. One miracle can fix everything. This thing about "order of difficulty" isn't just something that occurs in the first sentence of the Text. In fact, the phrase is repeated twenty-eight more times in the Course. The idea is obviously important. It's important, I think, because the concept of "order of difficulty" is deeply imbedded in our minds.

Miracles aren't just for difficult situations.

Whatever lies you may believe are of no concern to the miracle, which can heal any of them with equal ease. It makes no distinctions among misperceptions. Its sole concern is to distinguish between truth on the one hand, and error on the other. Some miracles may seem to be of greater magnitude than others. But remember the first principle in this course; there is no order of difficulty in miracles (T-2.I.5:1-5).

Here, we are being told that the miracle can heal any lie, any misperception with equal ease. Miracles apply to everything. Ironically, I think one of our major difficulties with miracles is that we only expect them to be necessary for *really difficult* problems, or problems that we perceive as incapable of resolution by "normal" means. Most problems we try to handle by ourselves, and that is precisely our biggest mistake. It's also one of the reasons we tend to think miracles are rare; we don't even look for them in most situations!

This concept is crucial to the Course.

To the Holy Spirit, there is no order of difficulty in miracles. This is familiar enough to you by now, but it has not yet become believable. Therefore, you do not understand it and cannot use it. We have too much to accomplish on behalf of the Kingdom to let this crucial concept slip away. It is a real foundation stone of the thought system I teach and want you to teach. You cannot perform miracles without believing it, because it is a belief in perfect equality (T-6.V(A).4:1-6).

I quote this passage mainly for two thoughts: First, the concept of no order of difficulty is *crucial* to the Course's thought system. This is not a side issue or sub-topic: "It is a real foundation stone." This is something we absolutely must grasp if we want to learn and teach Jesus' thought system. And second, we cannot perform miracles without believing it! That makes it really central, doesn't it, since miracles are the central topic of this course?

Miracles are meant for "all situations."

> Miracles demonstrate that learning has occurred under the right guidance, for learning is invisible and what has been learned can be recognized only by its results. Its generalization is demonstrated as you use it in more and more situations. You will recognize that you have learned there is no order of difficulty in miracles when you apply them to all situations. There is no situation to which miracles do not apply, and by applying them to all situations you will gain the real world (T-12.VII.1:1-4).

The learning we are going through, in studying the Course, is simply learning to apply miracles to more and more situations. The demonstration that we have learned something is that miracles happen for us and around us. If miracles are not happening, something is wrong. As Miracle Principle 6 says: "Miracles are natural. When they do not occur, something has gone wrong" (T-1.I.6:1-2). The goal of learning is reached when we have learned there is no order of difficulty in miracles, and the evidence that we have learned this is that we will apply miracles "to all situations."

Let's think for a minute about what we have said a miracle is: an activity of the Holy Spirit, in which He shifts our minds from false to true perception, from bondage to the laws of this world to the freedom of Heaven. Now how is that the solution to a bad hair day? What makes a bad hair day bad? Isn't it our perception? It isn't really high or low humidity or too much oil in our hair that causes us distress. It is our thoughts about our hair, our concerns about our hair as a tool for attracting the right bodies, or influencing people's opinions of us.

What the Course is telling us is that we need to apply miracles equally to everything. The solution to our problem, whatever that problem may be, is allowing the Holy Spirit to break up our false perception of the situation and to inject His perception into it.

We may not understand how doing that will alter the situation. The Course tells us that our understanding of how the miracle extends from our minds isn't necessary (in T-16.II.1:1-8). It will extend without our understanding. I don't understand everything about how my electronic mail reaches someone in Australia, but it does. Not understanding how it happens is a poor reason for not using it. But we try to make that a reason for not accepting a miracle as the solution: "How will changing my mind alter the fact that I still owe the rent and have no money?" The Course assures us that miracles *will* resolve all problems, if we will just start applying them to every problem that comes along.

Miracles simplify everything.

The idea of no order of difficulty means that the power of God offers the same solution to every problem; it sees all problems as the same, single problem.

> The power of God, and not of you, engenders miracles.... And being always maximal, it offers everything to every call from anyone. There is no order of difficulty here. A call for help is given help (T-14.X.6:9,13-15).

Consider how this resolves the imprisoning effect of having so many differing problems. First of all, they do *not* all require different solutions; the solution is a miracle. This simplifies everything. No longer do we have to beat our brains out trying to figure different solutions to different problems. One solution is enough for all of them.

Second, we no longer are baffled about how to find the time to solve all these various problems, because the miracle is the one solution to all of them. All we need to do is go for a miracle! All we need to do is turn to the Holy Spirit, accepting the fact that our disordered thinking is the sole cause of every problem, with just a little willingness to allow Him to dissolve our false perception of things, and to allow Him to reorganize our perceptions. Receiving the solution in one case will solve all the problems at once, if we are willing to recognize that they are all the same, and that the miracle applies to them all.

How do the miracle-minded live?

The more time I have spent studying what the Course has to say about there being no order of difficulty in miracles, the more I see that I have not really learned this. I have not learned to apply miracles to absolutely everything. Most of the time I never even think of asking for a miracle. Then, when something "big" comes up (big in my perception, not the Holy Spirit's), I don't have the habit of trusting Him to handle everything. Miracles are not natural to me. I panic. My first instinct, learned through long experience, is to start scrambling around trying to figure out a solution to the problem. I experience great anxiety because I think the solution is up to me. I expend huge amounts of energy trying to maintain my safety, instead of simply trusting in the miracle.

How would it look to live in this miracle-minded state of mind? In the Manual for Teachers, a teacher of God is described in the following way:

How simply and how easily does time slip by for the teacher of God who has accepted His protection! All that he did before in the name of safety no longer interests him. For he is safe, and knows it to be so. He has a Guide Who will not fail. He need make no distinctions among the problems he perceives, for He to Whom he turns with all of them recognizes no order of difficulty in resolving them. He is as safe in the present as he was before illusions were accepted into his mind, and as he will be when he has let them go. There is no difference in his state at different times and different places, because they are all one to God. This is his safety. And he has no need for more than this (M-16.7:1-9).

Thoughts for application

Think of a seemingly *difficult* situation confronting you. Repeat the words below (from Lesson 90 in the Workbook), applying them to this situation.

Then, think of some seemingly *minor* problem confronting you, and go through exactly the same process.

Try to remember, whenever any problem of any kind, large or small, in any area of life, arises: "The answer to this problem is the miracle that it conceals."
The answer is a miracle!

Let me recognize the problem so it can be solved.

Let me realize today that the problem is always some form of grievance that I would cherish. Let me also understand that the solution is always a miracle with which I let the grievance be replaced. Today I would remember the simplicity of salvation by reinforcing the lesson that there is one problem and one solution. The problem is a grievance; the solution is a miracle. And I invite the solution to come to me through my forgiveness of the grievance, and my welcome of the miracle that takes its place.

Specific applications of this idea might be in these forms:

This presents a problem to me which I would have resolved.
The miracle behind this grievance will resolve it for me.
The answer to this problem is the miracle that it conceals
(W-pI.rII.90.1:1-2:4).

-4-

Our Problems Are Too Big to Solve On Our Own; That Is Why We Need a Miracle

by Robert

4. We seem to be imprisoned by the size of our problems, by the fact that some problems are bigger and harder to solve.

One of the most basic facts of life as we know it is that problems come in different sizes. Some are massive; some too small to bother with. A dripping faucet can wait; a broken water main requires immediate attention. Therefore, we must set our priorities carefully. We must give more time and effort to the big problems, for they deserve more and usually *take* more. The big ones are generally much harder to solve; many of them seem impossible. Thus we all carry around in our minds a very long list of problems, and attached to each one is a degree of difficulty. That is how we know how to react to them. If you find out that you have an untied shoelace, you can react calmly, for this problem's degree of difficulty is extremely small. But if you find out that you have cancer, your emotional reaction is "necessarily" much bigger.

The big problems are of course the issue. All of us seem to lug around a private collection of really big, long-term problems that apparently defy solution. These become the walls of our personal prison.

4A. There is no order of difficulty in miracles.

This, of course, is the first principle of miracles, according to the Course. It means that miracles can heal any problem, no matter how seemingly big or small, with equal ease. A miracle can raise someone from the dead as easily as it can heal a headache. Many of us Course students have heard this first principle so many times that its meaning has probably worn smooth. Yet when you step back and really take it in, it is mind-boggling. It runs counter to our most fundamental assumptions about reality. Based on these assumptions, we assume that miracles might have a powerful effect in the case of psychosomatic illnesses, but not with genuinely organic illnesses, and especially not with terminal illnesses. But this first principle says otherwise. Just imagine walking around with the attitude that all of your problems can be solved for you with equal ease. How different that would be!

Because it so violates our current worldview, we might consider this principle irrelevant until the day that we reach some highly advanced state. Until then, we can safely file it away in the back of our minds as one of those "way-out" principles that probably makes sense from some higher perspective. The Course, however, takes a very different attitude:

> To the Holy Spirit, there is no order of difficulty in miracles. This is familiar enough to you by now, but it has not yet become believable. Therefore, you do not understand it and cannot use it. We have too much to accomplish on behalf of the Kingdom to let this crucial concept slip away. It is a real foundation stone of the thought system I teach and want you to teach. You cannot perform miracles without believing it (T-6.V(A).4:1-6).

Instead of filing this idea away, then, how can we make it more a part of us and so experience its results? Here are some suggestions drawn from the Course:

Simply remember the first principle.

Perhaps the most basic injunction is to just try to "remember the first principle in this course; there is no order of difficulty in miracles" (T-2.I.5:5). For most of us, just consistently doing this would be a big step forward.

Let there be no range in what you offer to your brothers.

> Only one equal gift can be offered to the equal Sons of God, and that is full appreciation. Nothing more and nothing less. Without a range, order of difficulty is meaningless, and there must be no range in what you offer to your brother (T-6.V(A).4:7-9).

According to this passage, if we want to realize the first principle of *A Course in Miracles*, we can focus on offering everyone the same gift of full appreciation. If we do this, the idea of order of difficulty in miracles will become meaningless, and we will begin to see miracles solving problems regardless of their seeming size and gravity.

Remember that God gives all His power to every miracle.

The reason the Course gives for there being no order of difficulty in miracles is that miracles "are all the same. All expressions of love are maximal" (T-1.I.1:3-4). Every miracle has maximal power, total power, and that is why it can raise the dead as easily as heal a headache. Miracles seem to be limited in their power only because we place limits on them. Therefore, it is helpful to remind ourselves that God gives all of His power to every miracle, as this passage says: "The power of God is limitless. And being always maximal, it offers everything to every call from anyone" (T-14.X.6:12-13). Notice the reasoning here. If God's power is truly limitless or maximal, every expression of it—every miracle—must also be limitless or maximal. Otherwise the power itself would be limited.

Realize that all illusions are equally undesirable.

The reason that the Course repeatedly gives for the apparent order of difficulty in miracles is that there are certain things we do not want healed. In other words, the size of a problem is not an objective property of that problem. It is a measure of how deeply attached we are to that problem. And that attachment is actually "a prayer the miracle touch not some dreams" (T-30.VIII.3:4). The Course makes this point over and over:

> When you maintain that there must be an order of difficulty in miracles, all you mean is that there are some things you would withhold from truth. You believe truth cannot deal with them only because you would keep them from truth (T-17.I.3:1-2).

While this makes a certain sense in the abstract, it suddenly appears quite strange when you apply it to your life. Think of the problems that you regard as the biggest and most insoluble. According to this theory, they are the ones you are most attached to keeping! How can we explain this? The only way is to remember the Course's teaching of the attraction of guilt, fear, and pain. The Course teaches that below the conscious level we have a deep attraction to various forms of suffering because these confirm our supposed existence as separate beings, as egos. By cementing our separateness, they protect us from the threat of losing our "identity" in the boundless One.

Therefore, to really experience the lack of order of difficulty in miracles, we must be willing to admit that we derive a certain twisted sense of safety from our problems. And we must be willing to surrender that in favor of a safety without walls and without boundaries.

Realize that healing is wholly desirable.

This is closely related to the preceding idea. The Course says that the reason we perceive orders of difficulty in healing is that "the ego perceives nothing as wholly desirable" (T-7.XI.1:7). If we perceived the healing of any particular problem as wholly desirable, the miracle could heal it with no difficulty whatsoever. So again, we have to address how much we truly want healing, and be willing to look at and give up our desires for something else.

Realize that all sickness and all problems are equally illusory.

The most frequent reason the Course gives for there being no order of difficulty in miracles is that all problems and all sicknesses are illusory. "There can be no order of difficulty in healing merely because all sickness is illusion" (M-8.5:1). To put this differently, all problems are merely different shapes and sizes of zero. And big or small, zero is still zero. It is nothing. Consciously remembering that all problems are empty nothingness dressed up as something can make the first principle of miracles more active in our experience.

Do not make distinctions among the problems you perceive.

If all problems are really nothing, then they are all the same. They therefore do not deserve different emotional reactions. Each one deserves the same neutral reaction accorded to the meaningless. The Course actively encourages this attitude: "He need make no distinctions among the problems he perceives, for He to Whom he turns with all of them recognizes no order of difficulty in resolving them" (M-16.7:5).

Let go of your judgments about the problems you perceive.

What makes problems seem different, according to the Course, is simply our judgments about them. These judgments may be based on "hard" physical evidence. Yet if physical matter is illusory, then physical evidence cannot tell us anything real. Therefore, it is only our judgments that make healing seem more available in some circumstances than others. "Yet it is when judgment ceases that healing occurs, because only then it can be understood that there is no order of difficulty in healing" (P-3.II.7:1). A central part of the acceptance of the miracle's full power, then, is consciously releasing our judgments about a particular problem.

Regard everything you see as equally meaningless.

Throughout the early Workbook lessons we are urged to be totally indiscriminate in selecting the things to which we apply the exercise. For instance, in Lesson 1 we randomly look around and say, "This _____ does not mean anything." This random application is said to be essential to the entire practice of the Workbook. Finally, in Lesson 19, comes this statement: " Lack of order in this connection will ultimately make the recognition of lack of order in miracles meaningful to you" (W-pI.19.4:3). In other words, if you regard all the physical illusions around you as being equally meaningless, you are implicitly affirming the miracle's complete power over all illusions.

Thoughts for application

To put some of these ideas into practice, you might want to think of what seems to be a particularly big problem in your life or in the life of someone you know. Notice how you currently perceive this problem. Notice the feeling of size and impenetrable solidity, how impervious it feels to change and how difficult you feel healing it would be. Then turn your mind to the following ideas, dwelling on each one until you feel it have an effect on your mind, and then going on to the next:

Let me remember that God gives all His power to the healing of this problem.

I have no need of this problem. It is wholly undesirable, whereas the healing of it is wholly desirable.

This problem has no reality whatsoever. That is why the miracle can heal it so easily.

Only my judgments about this problem make it seem more difficult to heal. I will let these judgments go now.

5. We apparently have to get out of prison through our own limited power and wisdom.

Our normal view, of course, is that we must solve our problems with our own strength and intelligence. Because our problems are so many, so varied and so large, our possible inadequacy for the task becomes an endless source of fear. We are afraid that we do not have enough time, energy, money, knowledge, ingenuity, intelligence, courage, experience, tools, contacts, initiative, willpower, skill, training, power, influence, maturity, etc. Pick any problem in your life and you probably have worries about your adequacy in several of the preceding areas. And that is frightening. You could even say that that is why fear exists. If we had enough of whatever it takes to solve any possible problem, how could we be afraid?

5A. The Holy Spirit delivers us. We don't have to.

A common response to our seeming inadequacy to solve our problems is to convince ourselves that we really are adequate. If we can gain enough confidence and skill, go to school long enough and attend enough self-help seminars, we can solve our problems, control our environment and master our destiny. The Course's response is dramatically different. It says, in effect, "Admit it—you just don't have what it takes." True, the Course has the most exalted notions of our true power. But it also teaches that we are currently in a state of profound alienation from that power. By choosing a condition of separateness, we have severed our awareness from our true Identity and its unlimited power.

Therefore, says the Course, we need miracles. We need an Emissary from our true Self, a Messenger Who can make active in our lives the power of that Self. This Emissary, of course, is the Holy Spirit. He is the One Who actually does the miracle. The miracle is His activity in us and through us. He is the One Who heals our minds for us.

This is why I take issue with the universal idea among Course students that the miracle is a shift in perception. I like this idea in that it affirms that the miracle's primary aim is the inner healing of perception, not the outer healing of bodies (though this results from inner healing). However, saying that a miracle is a shift in perception also carries the connotation that we are the ones doing the miracle, doing the shifting. And that is not how the Course talks. The Course never once calls the miracle a shift in perception. As Allen pointed out in Chapter 1, the Course talks about the miracle as some kind of impulse or catalyst from the Holy Spirit that acts upon our minds and heals our perception. Thus, rather than *being* a shift in perception, it would be more accurate to say that the miracle *shifts* perception.

The upshot of this is that we do not have to solve our own problems. The Course teaches that our faulty perception is the core of every problem we experience. And if a miracle is there to heal that perception, then solving our problems is not our job. A miracle is there to solve them for us. All we have to do is accept this miracle.

What a liberating concept! This is the age-old appeal of miracles. Something in us knows that our strength is not equal to the problems that confront us. We know we need a miracle. This also has been much of the appeal of *A Course in Miracles*, especially in its early days. However, as time has passed and our overall understanding of the Course has deepened, an unfortunate by-product has been to lose sight of this liberating concept of miracles. Yet this is a *course* in miracles. It is a course in how to experience release from everything that hurts and limits us. The Course wants us to feel the power of this promise and to claim it as our own.

Our Problems Are Too Big to Solve on Our Own; That Is Why We Need a Miracle

How, then, do we let the Holy Spirit give us a miracle? The simple answer is *that the miracle is done for us when we stop trying to do it for ourselves.* Our own persistent belief that we alone can solve our problems is an implicit shutting out of the Holy Spirit. Saying, "I can do it on my own," is another way of saying, "I don't need Your help, thank You very much." The following categories elaborate on this idea.

Realize that settling problems by yourself keeps them apart from healing.

These three passages express the exact same idea:

> And as we practice, let us think about all things we saved to settle by ourselves, and kept apart from healing (W-pI.193.11:4).

> To give a problem to the Holy Spirit to solve for you means that you *want* it solved. To keep it for yourself to solve without His help is to decide it should remain unsettled, unresolved, and lasting in its power of injustice and attack (T-25.IX.7:5-6).

> Would you first make a miracle yourself, and then expect one to be made *for* you? (T-18.IV.4:10).

It is remarkable how many times the Course says that our attempt to solve our own problems is what keeps them from being solved. We may solve them on an external level. But at the core of every external problem is an unhealed perception. So if we solve the external aspect but leave the core perception unchanged, it will simply give birth to another outer problem, and it will keep doing so until it is finally healed. This healing, however, is something we cannot do by ourselves, which is why none of our problems can really be solved by us.

Acknowledge that by yourself you could not solve your problems.

> How can you, so firmly bound to guilt and committed so to remain, establish for yourself your guiltlessness? That is impossible. But be sure that you are willing to acknowledge that it *is* impossible. It is only because you think that you can run some little part, or deal with certain aspects of your life alone, that the guidance of the Holy Spirit is limited (T-14.XI.8:1-4).

This passage says that under your own power you will never come to believe in your innocence. Why? Because you are "firmly bound to guilt and committed so to remain." Acknowledging this may seem like the road to despair, but it is actually the other way around. *Refusing* to acknowledge this is what shuts out the Holy Spirit and thus keeps your guilt unhealed and your problems unsolved. Paradoxically, admitting your powerlessness is the road to miracles. As the Manual states, "To say, 'Of myself I can do nothing' is to gain all power (M-29.4:2).

Refusing to solve your problems on your own invites the Holy Spirit.

By this refusal to attempt to teach yourself what you do not know, the Guide Whom God has given you will speak to you. He will take His rightful place in your awareness the instant you abandon it, and offer it to Him (T-14.XI.6:10-11).

These lines follow a practice we are given in the Text, in which we look at a "disturbing" situation and say, "I do not know what anything, including this, means." This certainly does not sound like a very empowering affirmation, yet according to the Course it is exactly that. For the simple refusal to interpret situations on your own and solve them by yourself is an invitation to the Holy Spirit. If you get out of the driver's seat, He will automatically step in.

Does this mean that you should never do anything toward solving your problems? Does it mean that you never gather any facts or entertain possible solutions? I personally think you do need to gather facts at times. But once you do I think you should step back, suspend your interpretations of what they mean, and tune into a higher interpretation that comes from deep within you. I also believe in trying to think creatively to solve problems. But again I think this should take place after you have tried to let go of the meanings you placed on the situation. Then you are more open to a wisdom that comes from beyond the limits of your personal mind.

A practice for letting Him solve it

It is not sufficient to simply "know" that trying to solve things on our own shuts out the Holy Spirit. For our minds are constantly and habitually trying to manage on their own. We therefore need specific methods by which our minds can stop this incessant struggle and put the reins in the Holy Spirit's hands. The following is one such method, drawn from "The Obstacles to Peace" in the Text. It is a particularly useful practice for when your mind is latched onto a painful interpretation, when seeing things differently seems like a complete impossibility. When this happens, focus on these words and try to join with their meaning:

Our Problems Are Too Big to Solve on Our Own; That Is Why We Need a Miracle

Take this from me and look upon it, judging it for me.
Let me not see it as a sign of sin and death,
*   nor use it for destruction.*
*Teach me how **not** to make of it an obstacle to peace,*
*   but let You use it for me, to facilitate its coming* (T-19.IV(C).11).

It can be very useful to memorize these lines so you can use them whenever you need to. Sometimes I use just the first sentence. However, I also find the third sentence particularly impactful. According to it, the Holy Spirit can show me how to see this situation in a completely different way. Under His guidance, what I experienced as a granite block to peace will suddenly become a *bringer* of peace. Now that is an amazing idea.

-5-
Miracles Are Mutual and Instantaneous

by Allen

6. We need to devote our power and wisdom to our own escape from prison. We might endanger our chances of escape by expending ourselves on the escape of others.

As we normally see it, we have a limited amount of power and wisdom available to us. Given the multiplicity and magnitude of all our problems, our own problems are more than enough; it would be foolish to try to help others as well. We don't have enough time for our own problems; we are not powerful enough and wise enough to solve all of them. How, then, could we be expected to take on the problems of others? So, as much as we want to be loving and helpful to others, we believe we are *forced* to focus nearly all of our attention on our own difficulties, and to let other people fend for themselves.

When for some reason we become unavoidably involved in someone else's problem, we resent it; we feel threatened because we have to stop paying attention to what we think is important, and divert our attention to the other person. This happens rather frequently in close relationships: marriages, family, friendships. For example, perhaps one person in the relationship is really working hard at some job or other, and the partner in the relationship gets upset because he or she feels ignored, as if the job were more important than they are. The first partner feels torn. "How can I do a good job if I have to pay attention to your problems? I have problems of my own at work!"

Most of the time we feel justified in ignoring other people's problems, or at least in giving them only a token effort. We are too involved in taking care of ourselves to be able to really give freely to others. Most of the time, people will even apologize for bothering you if they realize you are "going through something." Being wrapped up in your own problems has social approval.

But this actually is a form of imprisonment. Our freedom lies in one another. Relationships can be our salvation, and not our doom, teaches the Course. It is only as we recognize our shared Identity that we will truly know ourselves, because our reality is a shared reality. So, by not joining with others, although we do not recognize it, we are depriving ourselves, we are keeping ourselves from knowing our shared Identity as God's holy Son.

6A. The miracle benefits both giver and receiver. We receive through giving.

The miracle reverses the laws of this world. In the world, to give is to lose, and you gain by taking things. A miracle demonstrates the exact opposite: to take from others is to deprive yourself, and you gain by giving.

Miracles demonstrate that giving is receiving.

This aspect of miracles is clearly interpersonal; one person gives or extends miracles to another. Demonstrating and teaching that giving is receiving is one of the main *purposes* of a miracle:

> Miracles are teaching devices for demonstrating it is as blessed to give as to receive (T-1.I.16:1).

How do miracles demonstrate that giving is receiving? The Course tells us:

> Miracles are a kind of exchange. Like all expressions of love, which are always miraculous in the true sense, the exchange reverses the physical laws. They bring more love both to the giver *and* the receiver (T-1.I.9:1-3).

When you extend a miracle to another person, you are cooperating with the Holy Spirit in their mind to induce a shift in their perception of their problem. This strengthens the other person, and you find yourself strengthened in return. Any miracle is an extension of love, and giving love does not deplete love, it increases it. So, when you share a miracle, you learn that to give is to receive.

You can see right away how this releases us from the prison of our personal problems. When you offer a miracle to your brother, *you receive what you need by giving it.* You are saved from your own problems by helping others. So instead of being limited in the amount of help you can give, you are suddenly freed. The more you give, the more you receive. The more you offer strength to others, the stronger you become.

No wonder the Course places so much emphasis on this "giving is receiving" idea. Not only is the miracle the one solution to all of your problems; in extending it to others you learn that it is the one solution to everyone's problems. Miracles show us that we are truly one, and thus end the illusion of separation on which all the world's laws and customs are based. A miracle proves that no one loses and everyone gains.

The thought "I can't help others because I am too burdened with my own problems" is really a form of the idea that, in order for someone to gain, someone else has to lose. In this case, in order for my brother to be blessed, I have to give up something. The miracle reverses that law, it inverts that perception, and shows that the opposite is true: When my brother receives a miracle, so do I.

When we are embroiled in our own problems, we see ourselves as being in need. It seems like we have nothing to give. If, despite that feeling (which is false), we choose to give anyway, what we learn is that we *do have* something to give; we recognize the miracle we have already received through our willingness to give it. We begin to learn that the way to receive what we need is to give it away.

Giving miracles should be guided.

We should remind ourselves in this context of what I began to point out near the end of Chapter One: while we need to be ready to offer miracles everywhere and to everyone, the specific persons to whom we offer miracles—the ones who are seeking us—only the Holy Spirit knows, and will show to us. This is why one of the "Principles of Miracles" that open the Text says:

> Miracles are habits, and should be involuntary. They should not be under conscious control. Consciously selected miracles can be misguided (T-1.I.5:1-3).

A bit later, the Text adds:

> I am the only one who can perform miracles indiscriminately, because I am the Atonement. You have a role in the Atonement which I will dictate to you. Ask me which miracles you should perform. This spares you needless effort, because you will be acting under direct communication....
> ....Miracles you are not asked to perform have not lost their value. They are still expressions of your own state of grace, but the action aspect of the miracle should be controlled by me because of my complete awareness of the whole plan (T-1.III.4:1-4, 8:3-4).

The idea behind these cautionary words, I think, is that left to our own devices we can burn ourselves out, trying to respond to every call for help we are aware of. Since everyone in this world is constantly calling out for help, while we are still subject to the limitations of bodily existence, this is an impossible task. When I speak about giving being receiving, I want to emphasize that we are giving *miracles,* and not necessarily meeting needs in terms of *form,* although we will be often directed to do that. The "action aspect of the miracle" needs to be controlled by Jesus (or the Holy Spirit), or we will find ourselves expending "needless effort." We should *ask* which miracles to perform, and not consciously select them on our own, based on our evaluation of needs.

Giving miracles to others is how we receive them.

One of the reasons the Course seems confusing to us is that we haven't learned to stop thinking in terms of linear time and separation between minds. When we describe the process of a miracle, we talk in terms of time, of things that happen one after another: we receive a miracle; then we extend it; then it returns to us in increased measure. In reality, I think, it all happens at once.

The Course tells us that we can't give something until we have it, so, thinking in terms of linear time, it would seem that before we can give a miracle we have to receive one. The Course says that, too. But it also says that the way we receive miracles is *by giving them.* For instance:

> You will never give this holy instant to the Holy Spirit on behalf of your release while you are unwilling to give it to your brothers on behalf of theirs. For the instant of holiness is shared, and cannot be yours alone....Miracles are the instants of release you offer, and will receive (T-15.I.12:1-2,4).

"Miracles are the instants of release you offer, and will receive." You offer them, and then you receive them. As long as you are unwilling to share the miracle with your brother, you can't receive it for yourself. You can't receive a miracle *alone.* Your willingness to release your brother is identical to your willingness to be released yourself; they are the same thing.

The choice to offer a miracle *is* the choice to receive a miracle. It isn't two different choices; it is the same choice. The shift in perception in your mind which the Holy Spirit brings, the very thing that heals you, is the shift into a willingness to offer the miracle to your brother. "The problem is a grievance" (W-pI.90.1:5); that is what is blocking your reception of the miracle. So the removal of that grievance, the change of mind that is willing to share the holy instant with your brother, is what releases you: "The solution is a miracle" (W-pI.90.1:5).

> There is no miracle you cannot give, for all are given you. Receive them now by opening the storehouse of your mind where they are laid, and giving them away (W-pI.159.2:4-5).

If you look carefully at what the last sentence is saying, and reduce it to its grammatical essence, it says: "Receive [miracles] by opening your mind and giving them away." *Receive miracles by giving them.* Other passages say the same thing in other words:

> We will not recognize what we receive until we give it (W-pI.154.12:1).

> So would I liberate all things I see, and give to them the freedom that I seek. For thus do I obey the law of love, and give what I would find and make my own. It will be given me, because I have chosen it as the gift I want to give (W-pII.349.1:1-3).

You receive what you want to find, and make it your own, by giving it to others. You choose what gift you want to give, and because you chose it, it will be given to you. You give to your brothers the freedom that you are seeking for yourself, and that is how you receive it.

One passage fairly early in the Text attempts to clarify this confusion we have about whether receiving or giving comes first. It tells us:

> You cannot perform a miracle for yourself, because miracles are a way of giving acceptance and receiving it. In time the giving comes first, though they are simultaneous in eternity, where they cannot be separated. When you have learned they are the same, the need for time is over (T-9.VI.6:3-5).

"You cannot perform a miracle for yourself." That's very important to realize: You can't give yourself a miracle! Why not? "...because miracles are a way of giving acceptance and receiving it." Miracles are a way of giving; they involve someone else by nature of what they are. They are "an exchange" (T-1.I.9:1); they are "a service...the maximal service you can render to another" (T-1.I.18:1-2). Miracles *always* involve yourself and others; you can't receive a miracle alone. Every miracle you receive represents some opening in your mind to the rest of the Sonship, some recognition of our shared Identity.

Now, in time, "the giving comes first." In time, then, we give the miracle before receiving it, or so it seems. Our mind must open to our brothers, we must let go of our desire to withhold love from our brothers, and then love enters our mind. So *it seems* as though we give the miracle to another, and then receive it for ourselves. In eternity, however, the giving and receiving are "simultaneous" (T-9.VI.6:4). The giving is the receiving. Giving is how we recognize we have received.

We are able to bring healing to others by allowing our mind to be healed. And we are healed as we let the Holy Spirit teach us to heal (T-2.V(A).18:6). Receiving and giving are the same.

Forgiveness, truth's reflection, tells me how to offer miracles, and thus escape the prison house in which I think I live (W-pII.357.1:1).

One of my favorite anecdotes that illustrates this point is found in Ken Wapnick's account of the scribing of the Course. At one point, Jesus said to Helen, "How often have I answered 'help him' [referring to Bill Thetford] when you asked Me to help you?" (*Absence from Felicity*, p. 299) Extending miracles to others, helping others, is the way we can open ourselves to receiving our own miracles.

Thoughts for Application

Call to mind someone you know of who is asking for help. Try not to be distracted by the "form" that his or her asking might be taking, which might seem like attack. With that person or situation in mind, apply these thoughts, asking for a miracle for the person or situation as sincerely as you can:

As I offer miracles and love to [name the person or situation], I am receiving miracles and love.

No one can lose, and everyone benefits, when I offer a miracle to [name].

If I am willing for [name] to receive the holy instant, I can also share this instant with the Holy Spirit.

Miracle are the instants of release I offer to [name], and will receive.

7. We can only get out of these problems slowly, if at all—by using all of our power and wisdom, by focusing them on ourselves, by respecting the size and type of problem, and by carefully obeying the laws that are oppressing us.

We are imprisoned by our thoughts when we think that it will take a long time for us to escape from our problems. Thinking it takes a long time follows logically from several of the thoughts of the world we have already examined:

- If we are relying upon our own power and wisdom, the progress is bound to be slow (#5).
- If we are fighting many problems, each one of them is going to take a long time to resolve, in tiny increments (#3).
- If we believe the problems come in varying sizes, then perhaps little problems can be solved in a little time, but really big problems will— of course!—take a lot of time, and *huge* problems may never be completely resolved (#4).
- If we are forced to divert our attention from our problems to helping others, our problems will take that much longer to solve (#6).
- If we are bound by the laws of the world, we will be limited by those laws in their relationship to time; money will accumulate slowly (if at all) by natural increments; health will return gradually (if at all), and so on (#1).

Time itself limits us. We are not only imprisoned by the past that cannot change, we are held back by the very nature of time. We cannot speed time up; each moment continues the past into the future at a measured pace, as Shakespeare wrote: "Tomorrow and tomorrow and tomorrow creeps in this petty pace from day to day, to the last syllable of recorded time."

It's only "natural," then, for us to believe that solving our problems will take a long time.

Whenever we are thinking along these lines, we are acknowledging our imprisonment to time. We are not being miracle-minded. We are, in fact, choosing to postpone our salvation to an indefinite future, instead of expecting salvation now.

7A. Miracles deliver us in an instant. A miracle establishes "an out-of-pattern time interval not under the usual laws of time" (T-1.I.47:2).

Miracles Are Now.

> This course is not beyond immediate learning, unless you believe that what God wills takes time. And this means only that you would rather delay the recognition that His Will is so (T-15.IV.1:1-2).

That reference tells us that the only thing that prevents us from learning the Course *immediately* is our belief that "what God wills takes time." And believing that it takes time is really just our wish to delay the recognition that what God wills "is so," right now. That is just what we do with miracles.

> A miracle is *now*. It stands already here, in present grace, within the only interval of time that sin and fear have overlooked [that is, the present], but which is all there is to time (T-26.VIII.5:8-9).

"The miracle is *now*." The only time we can experience the miracle is now, in the present. And whenever we need a miracle, it is "already here, in present grace." The miracle is *always present*. It takes no time to bring it to us. A miracle is *now*. Any healing can only come in the present moment because the present moment is all there is of time, all we ever experience.

Earlier in this same section, Jesus has pointed out that time and space are both aspects of a single illusion. He says:

> If it [the illusion] has been projected beyond your mind you think of it as time. The nearer it is brought to where it is, the more you think of it in terms of space (T-26.VIII.1:4-5).

In other words, the more we are aware of our wish for separation from our brothers, the more we think of the separation in terms of space, or physical separation. But the more we have projected our wish for separation outside of our minds, the more we see the cause as being outside of us, the more we think of it in terms of time: "It will take a long time to reconcile with this person; it will take a long time to reach forgiveness."

In paragraphs 2 through 4, Jesus continues to point out that what we perceive as "the time it will take" is really the distance we want to keep between ourselves and our brothers. This is why, "You see eventual salvation, not immediate results" (T-26.VIII.2:7). Because we want space between us, we want *time* in which to drag out our forgiveness. But the space between us exists only *now*, not in the future; therefore, *now* is the only time in which that space can be overlooked. If we are afraid in some way of the forgiveness process, it is not some future loss we are afraid of; it is present joining.

> Therefore must it be that if you fear, there is a present cause. And it is *this* that needs correction, not a future state (T-26.VIII.4:7-8).

And this is the context in which he tells us, "For a miracle is *now*. It stands already here, in present grace, within the only interval of time that sin and fear have overlooked, but which is all there is to time" (T-26.VIII.5:8-9). What prevents us from receiving the miracle *now* is not time, but our resistance to union.

We want a little space between us and our brothers, and we project that space as the time it will take to be healed. We want "eventual salvation, not immediate results" because that keeps salvation at a distance from us. It keeps us from receiving it.

The miracle is an out-of-pattern time interval.
The Course tells us:

> The miracle abolishes the need for lower-order concerns. Since it is an *out-of-pattern time interval*, the ordinary considerations of time and space do not apply. When you perform a miracle, I will arrange both time and space to adjust to it (T-2.V(A).11:1-3, my italics).

> The miracle is a learning device that lessens the need for time. It establishes an *out-of-pattern time interval* not under the usual laws of time. In this sense it is timeless (T-1.I.47:1-3, my italics).

The phrase "out-of-pattern time interval," seen here in Chapters 1 and 2 of the Text, seems to mean approximately the same thing as what the Text later calls the "holy instant"; the Text does not introduce that term until Chapter 15. The miracle occurs in the present, in the *now*; the mind, therefore, must let go of its focus on the past and the future, just as in a holy instant. The miracle is always there, in the holy instant, but our minds must truly enter the present, letting go of the past and future, in order to receive it.

We need to start thinking miraculously, instead of being limited by the plodding pace of time. With miracles, there is no need for any time but the present instant. Miracles take no time. The following is from a passage about the holy instant, but it applies equally well to miracles:

> This lesson takes no time. For what is time without a past and future? It has taken time to misguide you so completely, but it takes no time at all to be what you are (T-15.I.9:1-3).

When I find myself mulling over a problem, recently I have started asking myself, "Am I willing for a miracle to solve this problem *now?*" "Am I willing for the Holy Spirit to rearrange my perception of this *right now* so that I see the miracle that the problem is hiding?" I won't say that I have experienced a lot of miracles as a result—yet. But I feel something shifting inside of me, something that is starting to break free from the bondage to time, and to the belief that any solution *must be slow.*

I have often spoken or written about the other side of the coin: the naive idea that we can transcend our egos overnight, or that we can learn to hear only the Voice of the Holy Spirit easily and without effort. The Course points out that we can, and do, procrastinate and postpone our salvation, and that we can, and do, underestimate the depth of our delusion. We have buried our wish for specialness in heavy layers of denial. We are insane and we do not know it. It *does* take time to uncover all that self-deception, because our resistance to it is deep. We are asked in the Course to be patient, and to be content with healing.

All that is true, and I still believe it. I think, however, that this flip side—the immediacy, the nowness of miracles—needs equal emphasis. After all, miracles are *miraculous*. So I am trying, in my own life, to cultivate more of the mind-set that expects miracles, that is open to an activity of the Holy Spirit that is an out-of-pattern time interval. I am trying to open my mind to accepting great leaps forward in time, so that healing and learning do not "have to" take a long time.

The miracle shortens time.
The miracle minimizes the need for time (T-1.II.6:1).

We may not be ready for instantaneous healing, but perhaps we can begin to realize that the need for time can be minimized, or shortened. If we are not ready for instantaneous healing, either physical, or mental, or spiritual, how about accepting *accelerated* healing?

> In the longitudinal or horizontal plane the recognition of the equal-ity of the members of the Sonship appears to involve almost endless time. However, the miracle entails a sudden shift from horizontal to vertical perception. This introduces an interval from which the giver and receiver both emerge farther along in time than they would oth-erwise have been (T-1.II.6:2-4).

We are literally propelled into the future by miracles. We "emerge farther along in time." We've all heard about saving a thousand years through a miracle, and so on; but how often are we actually *expecting* that sort of thing?

> The miracle thus has the unique property of abolishing time to the extent that it renders the interval of time it spans unnecessary. There is no relationship between the time a miracle takes and the time it covers. The miracle substitutes for learning that might have taken thousands of years (T-1.II.6:5-7).

Notice that the miracle *substitutes* for learning that might have taken thousands of years. In other words, it *is* possible to drag along over the centuries and millennia, millimeter by millimeter, and arrive at the goal. But a miracle can provide a jet-assisted takeoff and pack that learning into no time at all!

> The basic decision of the miracle-minded is not to wait on time any longer than is necessary. Time can waste as well as be wasted. The miracle worker, therefore, accepts the time-control factor gladly. He recognizes that every collapse of time brings everyone closer to the ultimate release from time, in which the Son and the Father are one (T-1.V.2:1-4).

That's what I've been trying to get at, that "basic decision not to wait any longer than necessary." That's the idea that is reflected in these lines from the Workbook:

> What need have I to linger in a place of vain desires and of shattered dreams, when Heaven can so easily be mine? (W-pII.226.2:3).

> I will be still an instant, and go home. Why would I choose to stay an instant more where I do not belong, when God Himself has given me His Voice to call me home? (W-pI.202.1:1-2).

There does seem to be *some* need for time, since the basic decision is not to wait on time "any longer than is necessary." So, apparently, some time is necessary. That seems hinted at in the following description of miracles:

> ...miracles, the device for shortening but not abolishing time (T-2.VIII.2:6).

Miracles shorten time, they don't abolish time. The idea that keeps coming to me, though, over and over, is, "Don't delay the process. Don't wait on time when waiting on time isn't necessary. Expect miracles!"

Thoughts for Application

What are some ways in which you have been thinking, "It will take a long time"? What are some areas in which you have been thinking, "It will be healed *eventually*, but not now"? What are some upsets that are always simmering in the back of your mind? Apply some of these thoughts to such situations:

57

God's grace is given me; I claim the miracle now in this situation.

Why would I delay one instant longer and remain in this upset? I will be still an instant, and go home.

In this situation, I do not want to wait on time any longer than is necessary.

Am I willing for a miracle to solve this problem now?

It takes no time at all to be what I am.

This is my holy instant of release.

-6-
Miracles Are Dependable

by Robert

8. We need a miracle, but miracles are so rare. We simply cannot count on one coming.

This, of course, is how we see miracles. We all have heard stories of the most amazing miracles, stories that seem to be absolutely genuine. Yet we do not normally expect such things to happen to us, especially not on a regular basis. Why? The answer, of course, is that we "know" that miracles are rare. They are supernatural, which means that be definition they are outside the natural order of things. And this automatically identifies them as infrequent. Consequently, though we may hope for a miracle, we do not *count* on one.

8A. Miracles are natural, being God's Will.

One of the Course's most basic principles about miracles—actually, principle #6—is that miracles are *natural*. The Course mentions this again and again (I count eleven times). This is a flat contradiction of the way we normally think of them. What does it mean to say that miracles are natural? When something is natural it is in harmony with the nature of things. It is an expression of the basic nature of reality. It is part of the natural order and so should be a regular event, not a freak occurrence. If miracles are natural, then, they are an expression of the natural order and should therefore be commonplace.

But how can miracles be natural? Their whole purpose is to momentarily overturn the laws of nature. We saw in Chapter 2 that in miracles "every law of time and space, of magnitude and mass is transcended" (T-12.VII.3:3). How can *that* be natural? Because, according to the Course, *nature is unnatural* (T-7.XI.1:5). If reality is unified, changeless spirit, then physical nature, with its separate bodies and dynamic processes, is profoundly unnatural. In short, nature is artificial. You could even say that it is man-made.

Miracles, on the other hand, are natural because, here in this artificial world, they are an expression of the true nature of things. They follow naturally from the way things really are. Thus, the more open our minds become to reality, the more natural miracles will seem to us, and the more common they will be in our experience. This, says the Course, is how it is meant to be. It is right there in miracle principle #6: "Miracles are natural. When they do not occur something has gone wrong" (T-1.I.6:1-2). The Course fully expects us to reach a state in which miracles go forth from us like floating seeds from a dandelion. These two passages give a sense of just how frequent miracles can be for us:

> There is no situation to which miracles do not apply, and by apply-ing them to all situations you will gain the real world (T-12.VII.1:4).

> Miracles are not in competition, and the number of them that you can do is limitless. They can be simultaneous and legion (T-14.X.3:1-2).

The following categories give various reasons from the Course for why miracles are natural:

Miracles are natural because they are God's Will.

"Miracles are in accord with the Will of God, Whose Will you do not know because you are confused about what *you* will" (T-7.X.8:1). If you believe in God, then you also believe that God's Will is the most powerful force there is. Now imagine that God's Will, the most powerful force in existence, is for you to have miracles. Imagine further that the physical laws that miracles overturn are not God's Will, but are mere reflections of your own impotent wishes apart from God. Your true will is the same as God's Will, and so miracles are *your* will, too. So miracles are the joint will of you and God, and nothing real stands in their way. If all this is true, would miracles be natural?

Miracles are natural because they are expressions of love.

In the Text, Jesus says, "I understand that miracles are natural, because they are expressions of love" (T-4.IV.11:11; see T-1.I.3). What is the logic here? Why are expressions of love natural? First, of course, for love to express itself is a very natural thing. Second, love itself is natural. This, however, does not mean what it may sound like. It may sound like a birds-and-the-bees sort of state-ment—that it is as natural for humans to fall in love as it is for birds to mate and lay eggs. But that is not the Course's perspective on why love is natural. In the Course's system, true, divine love (as opposed to romantic love) is natural be-cause it is the fundamental nature of ultimate reality, spiritual reality. If you are in touch with reality, then, your natural expression will be love, in the form of miraculous healing and upliftment.

Miracles are natural because the Holy Spirit knows how to fulfill His function perfectly.

Follow the Holy Spirit's teaching in forgiveness, then, because forgiveness is His function and He knows how to fulfill it perfectly. That is what I meant when I said that miracles are natural, and when they do not occur something has gone wrong (T-9.IV.6:1-2).

This passage claims to explain the statement (in miracle principle #6) that miracles are natural. They are natural, it says, because the Holy Spirit's function is to extend miracles (or forgiveness, which is the same thing), and He knows how to fulfill His function perfectly. Miracles could only be unnatural occurrences if the Holy Spirit was a bungler. And that is what we imply when we think we cannot count on a miracle happening. We are subtly affirming that the Holy Spirit is too incompetent to be depended on. Is that a reasonable position?

To our other self miracles are as simple and natural as breathing.
It may seem impossible for us to ever see miracles as natural. Yet the Course says that there is another self in us—our right mind—that has always seen them in this way. "This other self sees miracles as natural. They are as simple and as natural to it as breathing to the body" (T-21.V.3:3-4). Think of how natural breathing is to your body. Breathing is so natural that you do it without thinking. You are doing it right now. It is so natural that it is very hard to stop doing it for long. Now reflect on the idea that there is a place within you where accepting and extending miracles is just like breathing.

Miracles are natural because attacks are really calls for love and miracles are expressions of love.
The above-quoted passage about miracles being as natural as breathing continues: "They are the obvious response to calls for help, the only one [this other self] makes" (T-21.V.3:5). This other self in you sees every attack as a sincere call for help, a call for love. Its automatic response, therefore, is to give love, to extend a miracle. It does this as naturally as you would say "hello" in response to being greeted by a friend.

Miracles are natural because minds, being joined, can influence each other.
This same passage continues: "Miracles seem unnatural to the ego because it does not understand how separate minds can influence each other" (T-21.V.3:6). Isn't this how we think? We think, "Since our two minds are separate, how can healing be transmitted from my mind to yours?" The Course is saying just the

opposite: Since your two minds are one, it is perfectly natural for healing to pass from one to another.

To imagine this, you might picture "separate" minds as being different sectors of a lake. These sectors are separated by fishing nets. The nets mark a boundary, but water can still pass from one sector to another. Thus, if you drop a rock in one sector, the waves produced will naturally travel to the other sectors. Likewise, if you allow a miracle into your mind, its effects will naturally wash into the minds of others.

Thoughts for application

To put some of the above ideas into practice, think of a particular problem in your life, something it would take a miracle to solve. While holding this problem in mind, reflect on the following thoughts. To enhance their impact, you might want to reflect on each line separately, asking yourself if you can accept it as true, and then going on to the next.

> *If Love is here (though unseen by me),*
> *if miracles are natural expressions of love,*
> *and if my problem is a call for love,*
> *how can Love not offer me a miracle here?*

> *If the Holy Spirit's function is to give miracles,*
> *and if He knows how to fulfill His function perfectly,*
> *is it possible that the Holy Spirit does not know how to give me a miracle in this situation?*

> *My thoughts about this situation imply that I cannot count on a miracle here.*
> *But to my right mind miracles are as natural and simple as breathing.*
> *Which is saner, my current thoughts or my right mind?*

9. We need a miracle, but there is nothing we can do but wait for Divine whim to grant us one.

This idea seems to describe the situation we are in. We need a miracle. God knows, we need a heap of them. Yet it seems that we have to wait for them like a farmer waits for rain. We have to wait on whatever mysterious winds will bring the clouds our way and let the healing rain fall on our dusty, cracked earth. We have to wait for God to be in the right mood. It could happen tomorrow; it might happen next year. In the meantime, we might as well get off our rears and try to solve our problems ourselves.

Our situation, however, is a little worse than the farmer's, or so it seems. For our rain—the miracle—supposedly depends on our *faith* in its arrival. But how can we give our faith to something so undependable? The unreliable does not exactly inspire faith. Since our faith is required, however, we do our best to muster it up and forget about the odds that seem so impossibly against us. Yet this breeds a mounting fear of the emotional backlash we will experience when our faith is let down.

I remember in high school having a terrible crush on a certain girl. Since she was probably the most popular girl in the school, for her to become interested in me would truly have been a miracle. So I figured that enlisting God's aid was my only chance. I prayed every night for months on end for God to "give" me this person. I mustered all the faith as I could. I offered Him all kinds of deals. I promised to be a really faithful Christian—for life—if He would just grant me this one thing. Of course, it didn't happen. As a result, something in me concluded that this process of depending on God for a miracle was not the most reliable one.

Not all requests for miracles are quite as juvenile as mine was (and certainly mine was not the kind of "miracle" the Course is talking about). Yet we have all probably had somewhat similar experiences. We ask and ask. We try to have faith. And the miracle doesn't come. This whole process takes such an emotional toll that most of us feel stress just at the thought of asking for a miracle.

9A. Miracles are always there, awaiting our acceptance. We can train ourselves to accept them.

A Course in Miracles teaches that for every problem, the miracle that will solve it is already there, standing right next to the problem, waiting to heal it. We quoted a passage in Chapter 2 which said that miracles "stand in shining silence next to every dream of pain and suffering, of sin and guilt" (T-28.II.12:2). If miracles are already there, next to every one of our problems, what are they waiting for? Quite simply, they are waiting for us. They are waiting for our permission. Although the Holy Spirit *does* the miracle, it is up to us to *accept* the miracle. We may not do the miracle, but we do let it happen. Our daily experience abounds with examples of this general principle. For instance, we don't make water come out of the faucet—the water pressure takes care of that—but we do let it out by turning on the faucet.

This dual idea weaves together two aspects of how miracles have traditionally been seen. This is from the entry on miracles in *The Encyclopedia of Religion*:

The history of religions has preserved the record of miracles, that is, events, actions, and states taken to be so unusual, extraordinary, and supernatural that the normal level of human consciousness finds them hard to accept rationally. These miracles are usually taken as manifestations of the supernatural power of the divine being fulfilling his purpose in history, but they are also caused to occur "naturally" by charismatic figures who have succeeded in controlling their consciousness through visions, dreams, or the practices of meditation (Vol. 9, p. 542).

Notice these two ways of looking at the miracle. We can see it as the action of a divine being at work in the world. Or we can see it as caused by a charismatic figure who has trained his mind through spiritual disciplines. The Course is saying that both are true. We can state the Course's version of these two aspects in this way:

1. The miracle is the action of the Holy Spirit at work in our lives.
2. But we must give Him permission to do so. To give Him this permission (at least consistently) we must train our minds through the mind training program of the Course.

These two points seem to make sense, yet their implication is that we are not giving the Holy Spirit permission, and that this is what keeps us from experiencing the miracle. How can that be? We certainly feel like we want deliverance from our problems. To find an answer to this quandary, let us look at this passage from Lesson 76:

We have observed before how many senseless things have seemed to you to be salvation. Each has imprisoned you with laws as senseless as itself. You are not bound by them. Yet to understand that this is so, you must first realize salvation lies not there. While you would seek for it in things that have no meaning, you bind yourself to laws that make no sense (W-pI.76.1:1-5).

In Chapter 2 we looked at the laws which seem to bind us: the "laws" of physical health, the "laws" of relationship, the "laws" of religion. The above passage clearly states that we are not bound by them. Yet it also gives the reason why we *believe* that we are: We think salvation lies in them. Plainly put, while we seek our happiness in things of this world, we bind ourselves to the laws of this world. We are *voluntarily* obeying the laws of this world because we want to get something from them. Voluntary obedience for the sake of gaining a reward is a very familiar theme in our lives. If, for instance, you are intensely attracted to someone, you might find yourself obeying this person's every whim in the hopes that you will be rewarded with love and affection.

This, in fact, is how laws work (at least laws as we know them). A law makes a demand. It says, "Obey me and you will be all right, perhaps even rewarded. Disobey and you will be punished. At the least, you won't get the reward." These laws have no power to make us obey. But if we want what they offer, we will obey them. Let's say, for instance, that you get hired for a job and your boss says, "If you hop on one foot all day long while humming 'The Battle Hymn of the Republic,' I will give you a paycheck." If you want the paycheck, you are of course free to obey this ridiculous demand. However, you are equally free to simply walk out. The reason we feel so bound by the laws of this world is that we want this world's paycheck. Yet if we choose, we can just walk out.

To apply this to your life, think about some problem for which you want a miracle. Now ask yourself, "What am I hoping to get in this situation?" Be honest with yourself. What is the outcome that your thoughts and desires really gravitate to? Chances are that you want something that is of this world. Perhaps you want someone to change. Perhaps you want some material condition to change. These are outcomes of this world and they bind you to the laws of this world. You choose this bondage, because you want its rewards and because the two are a package deal. Now if the Holy Spirit comes along and says, "I will give you a miracle that will deliver you from both this bondage *and* its 'rewards,'" how much would you want it? Now, perhaps, the idea that you are not giving the Holy Spirit permission to grant you a miracle makes more sense.

A course in miracles

We have trained our minds to be habitually on guard against anything that threatens to take our toys away. Our minds are trained to chronically refuse the miracle. This refusal goes extremely deep. Therefore, we need to gradually train our minds in the opposite direction. We need a training program in how to consistently *accept* miracles. In short, we need a *course* in miracles.

Most of us are so accustomed to the Course's title that we do not reflect on what it really means. When we first heard it, however, it may well have struck us as incongruous. Miracles are thought to be spontaneous acts of the Spirit. Yet the word "course" suggests that we will be taught them, that we will be trained in them. As we said above, in the Course both things are true. Miracles are acts of the Spirit that we must be trained to accept. They are always waiting to come into our minds, but we must learn how to let them in.

To learn this does indeed require a training program. The broad strokes of this program are the use of the Course's three volumes. We study the Text, practice the Workbook, and extend to others as teachers of God (á la the Manual). Each step in this program leads us further into the experience of miracles. By studying the Text, we learn the thought system that makes miracles possible and natural. By practicing the Workbook, we practice consciously allowing miracles into our minds. Finally, as teachers of God (for whom the Manual was written), we extend miracles to others, and so reinforce them in our own minds. Thus, after studying miracles and then practicing them, we *do* them. We become miracle workers.

As I have mentioned before, in the early years following the Course's publication, everyone was excited about miracles. Now students don't seem to talk about miracles very much. This, I am sure, is due to several factors. One of them, I think, is that our initial enthusiasm for miracles was a bit superficial. We were hoping for miracles in a pretty conventional, external sense. As we got deeper into the Course we realized that this was not the Course's focus (we will discuss this in the next chapter). However, I think that another factor is that we weren't experiencing the kind of dramatic miracles the Course promises. Just like my high school experience, we were hoping for miracles that didn't materialize, at least like we thought they would. And this led to discouragement.

Yet miracles are still the Course's promise. They are what it claims to teach us right on its cover. They are what it urges us to claim as our right. Thus, if we approach the Course not as a quick fix, but as an authentic spiritual path, and if we sincerely and diligently follow its program, miracles should be our result. We should see insurmountable problems melt away. We should see ancient hatred transformed into present love. We should even see the sick healed and the dead arise. We should see the Course deliver on its promise.

-7-

Everyone Is Entitled to Miracles; Miracles Heal the Body, but Are for the Mind

by Robert

10. Miracles are given to the elect, those in God's special favor. So let's hope we can earn God's favor and be one of the elect.

The above thought is absolutely basic to our traditional thinking about miracles. As if it is not bad enough that miracles are so rare, the few miracles that do occur tend to happen to certain people. They happen to saints, to holy men, to those who stand extremely high in God's favor. And we are not part of that elite group. Our only recourse, then, is to try to earn our way into God's inner circle. And how much hope do we really feel for achieving this? Probably very little. So we naturally conclude that we might as well shelve the thought of relying on a miracle and set about solving our problems ourselves.

Implicit in such thinking is the idea that we must become deserving of miracles. This assumption runs very deep. It issues from our ingrained sense of guilt and unworthiness. The idea that we are undeserving of miracles and must somehow become worthy, is really a terrifying thought. Yet we all have this thought in our minds. Perhaps it is buried under a layer of newly-acquired Course concepts that say that we are God's holy Son and that God is incomplete without us. If these new concepts, however, had completely replaced the old beliefs in our unworthiness, then miracles would be as natural and easy to us as breathing. And for how many of us is this the case?

Think, for instance, about a particular problem in your life, something that could really use a miracle. Try completing this thought: "If I were more [some character trait that you seem to lack] I would really deserve a miracle in this situation." See if your mind has something to fill in that blank. See if there is some particular trait that would seemingly make you more worthy of a miracle in this situation.

Still thinking about the same problem, try to complete this thought: "If I were like [name of an especially miracle-worthy person] I would really deserve a miracle in this situation." Does your mind fill in a name here? If you were like Mother Teresa or the Dalai Lama, would you feel that you were more deserving of a miracle?

Chances are that you were able to fill in these blanks. If you could, it shows that you do carry the thought of being undeserving of miracles. If you couldn't fill in the blanks, then one of two things is true: Either you fully realize that you are completely deserving of miracles and you experience them constantly in relation to all problems, great and small, whether the problem is yours or another's; or, you have successfully hidden your sense of being unworthy of miracles deep in your mind, where it can continue to block your experience of miracles.

10A. Miracles are given to everyone equally because everyone is fully deserving of them.

A Course in Miracles takes care to overturn the ancient assumption that God plays favorites in the doling out of miracles:

> A miracle *is* justice. It is not a special gift to some, to be withheld from others as less worthy, more condemned, and thus apart from healing. Who is there who can be separate from salvation, if its purpose is the end of specialness? Where is salvation's justice if some errors are unforgivable, and warrant vengeance in place of healing and return of peace?
>
> Salvation cannot seek to help God's Son be more unfair than he has sought to be. If miracles, the Holy Spirit's gift, were given specially to an elect and special group, and kept apart from others as less deserving, then is He ally to specialness. What He cannot perceive [specialness] He bears no witness to. And everyone is equally entitled to His gift of healing and deliverance and peace (T-25.IX.6:6-7:4).

This remarkable passage bears close scrutiny. Central to the concept of justice is impartiality. Justice is blind, meaning that it treats everyone the same. It grants no special favor. Whether you are rich or poor, white or black, powerful or homeless, true justice will treat you impartially and give you a fair trial. The Course takes our concept of justice and carries it to its logical extreme. It says that if justice truly treats everyone alike, how can it treat people differently according to their *behavior*? At the heart of our justice system is the idea that if you did a certain behavior, you are condemned, but if you did not do that behavior, you are set free. Our justice, therefore, does not treat everyone the same. If you didn't do it, you get treated differently. And that is a violation of the total impartiality of true justice.

How can the Holy Spirit work this way? If He gave miracles "specially to an elect and special group," He would be adding His omnipotent power to a system of separation and specialness. He would be helping mankind be even "more unfair than he [mankind] has sought to be." What an irony! He would be an "ally to specialness." He would stand at the head of a system of special favor. In short, He would be the King of injustice. And how could that save us from the injustice of the world?

In truth, the Holy Spirit knows nothing of specialness. He cannot perceive it and "He bears no witness to" it (note the trial language here). He treats everyone exactly the same, the rich and the poor, the black and the white, the "criminal" and the upstanding citizen. He sees everyone as "equally entitled to His gift of healing and deliverance and peace." He sees all individuals as fully deserving of miracles.

How can everyone be equally deserving? Our whole concept of deserving has to do with how virtuous one's behavior has been, and behavior differs from person to person. To the Holy Spirit, however, we are deserving not because of what we have done, but because of who we *are*. We are God's Son. We are perfect, boundless spirits, direct extensions of God, who are only dreaming that we are human beings. Our dreams may be different, but as dreamers we are exactly the same. We are deserving because of who we are as dreamers, not because of what we are dreaming.

For instance, imagine that St. Francis had a dream in which he killed an animal. Not only would such a thing be very uncharacteristic for him to do, he didn't really do it at all. He just dreamt it. Would we evaluate what St. Francis deserves based on who he is, or based on what he did in that strange dream? Our answer about St. Francis is the same as the Holy Spirit's answer about us. He does not care what we are dreaming, for He knows the true identity of the dreamer. We are the Son of God. And that is why we are entitled to miracles.

This idea that we are entitled to miracles is so essential, and so different from our conventional frame of mind, that the Course devotes a Workbook lesson to it. Workbook Lesson 77, "I am entitled to miracles," is one with which almost every Course student is familiar. Its purpose is to help us gain the confidence that miracles are our right. The lesson begins with teaching that tells us over and over that miracles are our right:

> Your claim to miracles....was ensured in your creation, and guaranteed by the laws of God.
>
> Today we will claim the miracles which are your right, since they belong to you. You have been promised full release from the world

you made. You have been assured that the Kingdom of God is within you, and can never be lost. We ask no more than what belongs to us in truth (W-pI.77.2:1,5; 3:1-4).

Note all the words that express how certain your entitlement to miracles is: *claim, ensured, guaranteed, right, belong, promised, assured.* This is strong language, yet this is how you are supposed to think. The Course really wants you to internalize the idea that miracles are your right, a right fully guaranteed by God Himself. To help you do so, this lesson then gives you a practice with this aim. You begin the practice "by telling yourself quite confidently that you are entitled to miracles" (4:1). Then, it tells you, "after this brief introductory phase, wait quietly for the assurance [from the Holy Spirit] that your request [for miracles] is granted" (5:1). The exercise, then, is a two-pronged approach to gaining the confidence that you are entitled to miracles. The first prong is affirming this confidence to yourself. The second prong is waiting for the Holy Spirit to give you this confidence.

Believing that we are entitled to miracles is essential, for without this belief we will inevitably try to make ourselves deserving of miracles. We will try to make ourselves holy so that we are worthy of receiving them. And this, says the Course, actually blocks them from our experience. The well-known section "The Little Willingness" (T-18.IV) discusses this. Its main focus is on trying to make ourselves worthy of the *holy instant,* but because of the close connection between miracles and the holy instant, we can apply its message to the miracle as well (which the section itself does in three places).

In many ways this section repeatedly says the same thing. The following list is my paraphrasing of what this section says about receiving the miracle:

In order to receive the miracle

- Don't try to achieve on your own the state of holiness its coming brings with it.
- Don't rely on your good intentions to bring it to you. The miracle's purpose is to give you holy intentions.
- Don't try to chase all the shadows out of your mind. That is the miracle's purpose.
- Don't try to make yourself worthy of it. Its job is to reveal your worth.
- Don't try to prepare yourself for it, to make yourself ready. Its job is to restore to you your awareness that you are eternally ready.
- Don't try to make a miracle for yourself. Just receive the miracle.

- Don't try to atone. It brings you the Atonement.
- Don't try to purify yourself. Its job is to purify your thoughts for you.
- Don't try to answer your own question. Just ask the question. The miracle is the answer.
- Don't try to release yourself from guilt. The miracle releases you. Just release yourself to the Giver of release.

The above ideas should make it abundantly clear why trying to make yourself worthy blocks the miracle. The miracle's job is to reveal your pre-existent worthiness. Trying to make yourself worthy to receive it is like trying to heal yourself to be worthy of visiting the doctor. If, in the midst of your efforts at self-healing, the doctor were to make a house call, what would happen? Either you would be too consumed with your self-healing process to let him treat you, or you would tell him, "Not now. I am not worthy of you yet. Please leave until I can be deserving of your gifts." Either way, the fact that you are trying (unsuccessfully) to do his job for him effectively shuts him out.

Thoughts for application

There is a beautiful application of the above thoughts in the section I have just been discussing, "The Little Willingness." There we are given a practice for *receiving* the holy instant (as opposed to trying to make ourselves worthy of it). This is one of the longer such practices given in the Text and includes one particularly long, bulky sentence. It is tempting, therefore, to just pass it over. However, I have found it to be very effective for letting in the realization that we are worthy of God's Presence. The specific focus of the practice is on receiving God into our minds in the holy instant. However, when God enters our minds, miracles naturally come along with Him. So this practice is closely connected with receiving miracles as well.

I recommend that you repeat the following lines very slowly, trying to mean them as much as you can. Let each line sink in before going on to the next.

> *I who am host to God am worthy of Him.*
> *He Who established His dwelling place in me*
> *created it as He would have it be.*
> *It is not needful that I make it ready for Him,*
> *but only that I do not interfere with His plan*
> *to restore to me my own awareness of my readiness,*
> *which is eternal.*

71

I need add nothing to His plan.
But to receive it, I must be willing
 not to substitute my own in place of it (T-18.IV.5:9-13).

I find that if I go through this several times it produces a definite sense of being open to God's Presence in my mind. I would recommend not only spending ten or fifteen minutes with it at a time, but also memorizing it so that you can use it whenever you want, without having to open your eyes to read it.

11. Miracles deliver us from the physical, yet this subtly imprisons us by affirming that the physical is cause and we are its effect.

In conventional thinking, the purpose of the miracle is to save you from external problems, from sick bodies and ailing bank accounts. While such deliverance can feel exhilarating, it has a dark side to it. Let's say that you get delivered from some physical problem; say, an illness. You certainly feel better, but aren't you still left with the same inner problems you had before? At the heart of these inner problems, in the Course's view, is your belief that the outer world is the cause of your unhappiness. You see yourself as a little mind at the mercy of a big world, a world whose winds of fortune have the power to make you happy or make you miserable. The "miracle," by aiming its healing at one of your outer problems, has played right into this belief system. Now, even though this one problem is solved, you find yourself surrounded by a multitude of other problems whose power to make you suffer has just been strengthened in your mind.

You can probably think of examples of this very process in your life. Perhaps you haven't been cured by what you would consider a miracle. But think about when your body has been healed by medicine. Did it really solve your problems? Or did it just remove *one*, in the process reinforcing your belief that your outer problems *are* the problem?

11A. Miracles deliver us from our insane perceptions. They release us from the prison of this world by showing that only mind is cause and that the external world is an unreal effect.

As nearly every Course student knows, the purpose of miracles is to heal our perceptions. For it is our perceptions that make us happy or unhappy. This is the most basic of Course principles, but it cannot be emphasized enough. As much as we Course students know that changing our perceptions is the path to salvation, we still expend our energy every day rearranging external situations in order to feel better. I can't count how many times I have seen someone (including myself) finally solve a painful outer condition in his life, only to find that his mind now fixated on a new set of problems. He was really no happier than he was before the problem was solved. The real problem was in his mind, in his perception, which had remained essentially unchanged.

However, as most Course students also recognize, the miracle does not stop with the healing of perception. It does have effects on the external world. Many times, for instance, the Course talks about miracles healing the body (we will examine one soon). What is extremely confusing for Course students is the relationship between the miracle's healing of perception and its healing of outer form. How can the miracle heal both inner and outer? And why would it even touch the outer world if that world is only an illusion? I discussed this relationship already in Chapter 2, yet it is such a source of confusion that I would like to discuss it again, using a passage that I also referenced in Chapter 2. This passage comes from "Reversing Effect and Cause," Section II of Chapter 28:

The miracle returns the cause of fear to you who made it (11:1).

This means that the miracle shows that your fear is not being caused by outer problems. It is being caused by your own decision; in particular, your own belief in guilt. Your outer problems are the effects of this internal guilt.

But it also shows that, having no effects, it is not cause, because the function of causation is to have effects. And where effects are gone, there is no cause (11:2-3).

The miracle wipes away the effects of your guilt. It wipes away the problems and sicknesses that seemed to cause you fear. Now your guilt has no effects. And if it has no effects, it cannot be a cause. How can there be a cause that doesn't have any effects? And if your guilt is not a cause, it must be nothing. For everything real has power to cause something.

Thus is the body healed by miracles because they show the mind made sickness, and employed the body to be victim, or effect, of what it made (11:4).

Here it is clearly stated: "The body [is] healed by miracles." You can't get any more straightforward than that. Miracles heal the body. In the process, they show that illness originated in the mind, and that the mind then used the body as the projection screen for its mental illness. How do miracles show this? Apparently, they show it by reversing the process. The miracle heals the mind and this healing releases the body from the sickness the mind laid on it. This sounds like concepts that you could read in a variety of spiritual sources: Just as the mind's sickness made the body sick so the mind's healing makes the body well. Yet now this passage takes a dramatic turn:

> Yet half the lesson will not teach the whole. The miracle is useless if you learn but that the body can be healed, for this is not the lesson it was sent to teach (11:5-6).

That the miracle can heal the body is only half of the lesson. And the miracle is actually useless if you stop with this first half, for it was sent to teach your mind the whole lesson. What is the lesson?

> The lesson is the *mind* was sick that thought the body could be sick; projecting out its guilt caused nothing, and had no effects (11:7).

This sentence tells us the lesson the miracle was sent to teach us, yet it is a hard sentence to fully understand. Let us take it one part at a time. First, the lesson is that "the *mind* [as opposed to the body] was sick." What was the nature of the mind's sickness? The mind's sickness lay in a warped belief, the belief that "the body could be sick." How is it a sick belief to think that a body can get sick? Bodies get sick all the time. The answer: "Projecting out [the mind's] guilt caused nothing, and had no effects." According to the Course, projecting out the mind's guilt is what causes sickness. Yet here this projection is said to cause *nothing*, to have *no* effects. This can only mean that sickness *itself* is nothing, which must mean that the body is also nothing. How can the body be real when its sicknesses are unreal? Thus, the belief that a body can be made sick is *itself* a sickness. It is a sick belief.

So what is the lesson the miracle was sent to teach? It was sent to teach us the following:

1. The mind became sick with guilt.
2. It then projected this guilt onto the body, causing physical illness.
3. This projection of guilt, however, caused nothing real, since the sickness and the body are both illusory. And if the mind's guilt caused nothing then that guilt must itself be nothing.
4. Yet the mind believed that its projection caused something real, and this belief is part of its sickness. The mind's sickness is not only the cause of physical illness, it is the belief that in causing that illness it really caused something.

Everyone Is Entitled to Miracles;
Miracles Heal the Body, but Are for the Mind

I realize that this is a fairly complex set of ideas. But they hold the key to the relationship between the miracle's healing of the mind and its healing of the body. The following paragraph captures how I see that relationship, as plainly as I can put it.

You receive a miracle. This heals the mental illness that was the hidden projector of a bodily illness. With its projector turned off, the bodily illness vanishes. This disappearance sends a message to that deep part of your mind that was causing your physical illness. It says, "See, you didn't really cause anything. What you thought you caused (the physical illness) must have been very flimsy and insubstantial to so easily disappear. It must never have been real in the first place. In the empty space it vacated you are now looking upon its true nature. For it was nothing. And so the guilt that caused it must also have been nothing. Thus, you never really sinned. And you never really made a sick body. You did nothing at all. Having done nothing, you are still as God created you. And now you can finally realize that, now that the miracle has undone what you thought you did."

These ideas are encapsulated in this profound but puzzling line found earlier in the same section of the Text: "The miracle does nothing but to show him that he has done nothing" (T-28.II.7:10). By wiping away the outer effects of our supposed sins—our sicknesses and problems—the miracle shows us that those effects were unreal, and that our sins were unreal as well. This may not be the effect the miracle has on us *consciously*, but I think this is the effect it has on that buried, guilt-ridden part of our mind that believes it has sinned and has projected a real illness onto a real body. In the wake of the miracle, that deep part of our mind becomes absolved. The miracle has undone what it thought it did, and thus has demonstrated that it did nothing.

The whole purpose of a miracle, then, is to heal the mind. It heals the perceptions which manifest as our outer difficulties. And by wiping away those outer difficulties, it heals our belief that we manifested something real. It does heal external forms, but only so that it can teach our minds the unreality of all that we thought we did.

-8-
An Appreciation of the Fifty Miracle Principles

by Robert

T*he following are restatements of the fifty miracle principles. Rather than attempting to directly restate the principles and literally capture their meaning, my purpose is to draw out the sense of liberation contained in the principles. You may want to read each principle in the Text before reading my "appreciation" of it.*

1 & 49. Nothing stands in the way of the miracle's maximal healing power. It corrects all misperceptions no matter how "big" they are and is not even capable of distinguishing between them.

2. Miracles are purely a means for re-awakening you to their Source and your Source. They require no homage as ends in themselves.

3. Love by its very nature effortlessly and naturally expresses itself. Its expression is the miracle. Miracles naturally come from love as perfume from flowers.

4. God gives the miracle, for it is the gift of life. Because He gives miracles, you need not worry about how, when, or to whom to give them. He will tell you.

5. Miracles should be involuntary habits that just happen through you, not anxious accomplishments manufactured by the strain of your will.

6. Miracles are completely natural and should be the rule, not the exception.

7. Everyone has a right to miracles. They need only claim this right through the purifying of their thoughts.

8. Even when you perceive yourself in lack and can seemingly do nothing about it, there are those around you who have miracles and can give them to you, thus supplying your lack.

9 & 16. There would be an impediment to miracles if the giver of them had to make a sacrifice in giving them. Yet he does not. By giving them, he too gains, along with the receiver. And thus he also gains the understanding that giving and receiving are one.

10. Miracles aren't spectacles whose agenda is to coerce you into acknowledging how great God is. They just give. They just release.

11. You must have love to express it. Yet this love is freely given by God through prayer.

12 & 36. Miracles are within reach because they are thoughts, and your mind has the power to accept either thoughts of the body or miraculous thoughts. Miracles are thoughts of truth you share with the Holy Spirit. They align your perception with truth.

13. Miracles hearken back to the pristine beginning and forward to the eternal end. In an instant they undo the past that stands between these two, releasing you to a new future.

14. Miracles are not a hollow display of magical powers. They are a transmission of one mind's conviction in the truth to another mind, who now will share the blessing of this conviction.

15. Every day and all of time should be devoted to miracles. That is time's only purpose. And that is how abundant and available miracles are.

16. See #9.

17 & 20 & 29. Identification with the body and its "reality" is what imprisons you. Miracles don't work within this prison system; they transcend it. They suddenly shift your perception away from the prison of bodies to the freedom of the spirit. That is how they heal.

18. In giving a miracle you have the privilege of maximally serving your brother and realizing his ultimate worth, while in the process discovering your own worth.

19. Miracles unite the Sonship because they depend on the laws of eternity, of oneness, not the laws of time and separation.

20. See #17.

21. In miracles you give the miraculous release of forgiveness to others. And in so doing you accept it for yourself.

22. The only reason to fear miracles is you believe that what they dispel can be protected from miracles forever. And it can't.

23 & 30. Miracles turn your perception right-side up, since having your perception upside-down is what made you sick. This gives spirit the place it belongs, where it can heal you.

24. Nothing stands in the way of miracles, not even sickness and death, simply because of the greatness of your power. Your power is so great that you made sickness and death. That is why you can abolish them. Your power is so great that you can create in the likeness of your Creator. Yet only what you create with Him is real. The rest is just an unreal nightmare. That is why your power can so easily dispel it.

25. The freeing power of miracles is at work every moment, as well as in the past and future, continually leading to the ultimate end of perfect and universal salvation.

26 & 28. All miracles do is undo your fear. They free you from the prison of fear. In this way they are a means to entering into revelation, where fear is already and completely abolished.

27. Jesus considers it an untold privilege to be able to pass on God's blessing to literally all of his brothers.

28. See #26.

29. By offering a miracle to another you simultaneously praise God and praise the perfection of His creations, your brothers. By praising your brother you heal him. See also #17.

30. See #23.

31. Miracles honor your holiness, revealing the innocence that can never be lost, allowing you to thank God for what you are.

32. Miracles do for you what you can't do for yourself. On behalf of your holiness they step between it and your unholy perceptions. They reconcile the two by making your perceptions perfectly holy. They therefore raise you beyond the prison of earthly laws to the realm in which you are already holy and perfect.

33. Miracles honor your true worth for you when you can't see it for yourself. They thus wipe away your loveless perceptions of yourself, releasing you from the imprisonment of your nightmares about yourself and restoring you to sanity.

34. Miracles make up for your lack and weakness, restoring your perfect inner strength, which gives you perfect protection.

35. Miracles express love and *bring* love, whether you can see their effects or not.

36. See #12.

37. A miracle enters your thought system from outside of it, dispelling false perception for you, giving you healed perception, making it possible to know the Divine Order again.

38. The Holy Spirit, not you, does miracles. He does them by His ability to separate out your illusions from the truth and see both for what they are.

39. Because He sees your illusions in light of truth, He sees them as completely false and vacuous. Thus His miracles dissolve your illusions as light banishes darkness.

40. The miracle lets you see the mark of God in everyone, showing you that everyone is part of His family, making everyone your brother.

41. Miracles correct your perception of lack, leading you to perceive only wholeness and completion.

42. Miracles in their strength release you from seeing yourself as weak, alone and deprived.

43 & 44. You need simply get in touch with the Christ within you and His

Atonement and you will be in a state of miracle-mindedness. In this state, miracles will come forth from you naturally.

45. A miracle is never without positive effect. It can heal anyone, regardless of their physical proximity to you and irrespective of the size of their difficulty.

46. Miracles are only temporary communication devices, being meant to restore you to that which is far beyond them: direct and total communication with God.

47. The miracle releases you from the confinement of time's slow march from one point to another. It literally shortens your stint in time.

48. The miracle allows you to actually control time.

49. See #1.

50. By comparing everything you made with the truth, the miracle releases you from all falsehood in which you ensnared yourself.

-9-
What the Miracle Worker Can Do

by Robert

I n this chapter I want to explore some of the remarkable things the Course says the miracle worker will be able to accomplish. The things we will be examining may sound utterly impossible. The Course, however, fully expects its students to be walking around performing miracles like these. Thus, even though such miraculous deeds may seem absurdly out of our reach, we can view them as promises of what we will experience as we truly practice the Course and advance along its path.

Your state of mind can shine into another mind, awakening your state in that mind.

The basic function of a miracle worker is to accept miracle-mindedness into his own mind and then extend that state into the minds of others. This idea is mentioned again and again in the Course:

> Because the miracle worker has heard God's Voice, he strengthens It in a sick brother by weakening his belief in sickness, which he does not share. The power of one mind can shine into another, because all the lamps of God were lit by the same spark. It is everywhere and it is eternal (T-10.IV.7:4-6).

> The sick must heal themselves, for the truth is in them. Yet having obscured it, the light in another mind must shine into theirs because that light *is* theirs (T-12.II.1:6-7).

In both of these passages, the miracle worker's state of mind shines into another's mind and becomes that mind's new state. Now, like the mind of the miracle worker, this person's mind is filled with light, permeated with God's Voice, and freed of the belief in sickness. This may seem hard to swallow. You may think that your state of mind has only a minimal effect on others. However, if you were truly in your right mind, your effect on others would be literally life-changing:

You *are* responsible for how [your brother] sees himself. And reason tells you it is given you to change his whole mind, which is one with you, in just an instant (T-21.VI.7:5-6).

You can heal the sick and even raise the dead.
The traditional image of a miracle worker is one who goes around healing the sick and raising the dead. That is, after all, what Jesus did. But is that what the Course means when it talks about miracles? Absolutely. The Course mentions many times that miracles heal the sick and even raise the dead. Here is one of those places:

> Miracles enable you to heal the sick and raise the dead because you made sickness and death yourself, and can therefore abolish both (T-1.I.24:1).

Your state blesses everyone you meet or who thinks of you.
When we think of healing going forth from us to another, we usually think of a physical interaction with that person. This, of course, will often be the case. But the Course is quite clear that physical contact need not occur. If separation is an illusion and minds really are joined, then healing *will* travel directly from one mind to another. It is inevitable. Once we reach a certain level of development, someone only needs to think of us, or we of them, to receive healing from us:

> From this day forth, your ministry takes on a genuine devotion, and a glow that travels from your fingertips to those you touch, and blesses those you look upon. A vision reaches everyone you meet, and everyone you think of, or who thinks of you (W-pI.157.5:1-2).

You can heal people across the world you never intended to heal.
Your healing is not limited to those who think about you or whom you think about. It extends to people all over the world, people you will never meet and whom you have no intention of healing. Imagine someone across the world stuck in a problem she seemingly cannot resolve. Suddenly, her shackles fall away, both within her and outside of her. She perhaps rightly attributes this to God, but she will never know the full story: that her deliverance came from the healing in your mind. According to the Course, this kind of thing is happening all the time, including while we practice our Workbook lessons:

> The Holy Spirit will be glad to take five minutes of each hour from your hands, and carry them around this aching world where pain

and misery appear to rule. He will not overlook one open mind that will accept the healing gifts they bring (W-pI.97.5:1-2).

You can heal animals and natural systems.

The healing that travels from your mind to distant places does not confine itself to human beings. According to the following passage, it will also heal wounded birds and even dry streams: "Each hour that you take your rest today, a tired mind is suddenly made glad, a bird with broken wings begins to sing, a stream long dry begins to flow again" (W-pI.109.6:1). If you think about it, this kind of thing could inspire a whole new kind of ecology movement.

You can literally move mountains.

If you thought the power promised to the miracle worker was sounding a little way-out, it now starts getting really outrageous. We are all familiar with Jesus' sayings in the Bible about the power of faith to move mountains. Personally, I always wondered if he meant such sayings literally or was just using colorful language for effect. In the Course he leaves no doubt about which is the case:

> It is hard to recognize that thought and belief combine into a power surge that can literally move mountains. It appears at first glance that to believe such power about yourself is arrogant, but that is not the real reason you do not believe it. You prefer to believe that your thoughts cannot exert real influence because you are actually afraid of them (T-2.VI.9:8-10).

This passage directly addresses our mind's tendency to shy away from thinking that we can literally move mountains. It not only says "literally," it even addresses our thought that it is "arrogant" to believe we can actually move mountains. This thought, it says, is a cloak which covers our real reason for doubting our power. This is our fear that our destructive thoughts pack more gun powder than we would like to believe.

In case your eyes gloss over this passage, the Course includes a similar one many chapters later:

> Why is it strange to you that faith can move mountains? This is indeed a little feat for such a power. For faith can keep the Son of God in chains as long as he believes he is in chains (T-21.III.3:1-3).

Here again Jesus directly confronts our doubts about the ability of faith to move mountains. He even says this is "a little feat" compared to another thing that faith can do. For our faith (in the ego) can actually keep the Son of God (which is ourselves) in chains. If God is infinitely powerful, then His Son must also possess unimaginable power. Keeping the all-powerful Son of God in chains, therefore, is a far greater feat than moving a mere mountain.

The Course, then, is saying that we really do have this power within us. And why wouldn't we? According to its teaching, our minds made those mountains in the first place, and even now are holding them in place.

You can have all power in Heaven and earth.

Most of us in the Western world are familiar with the biblical idea that Jesus was given all power in Heaven and earth after he ascended. Though this is a rather vague idea, one must admit that having all power in both earth *and* Heaven must amount to an awesome quantity. In the Course, Jesus confirms the notion that he has all power, but he does add an important additional idea: that he will give *us* all power when we reach the state that he has:

> [The Holy Spirit] has established Jesus as the leader in carrying out His plan since he was the first to complete his own part perfectly. All power in Heaven and earth is therefore given him and he will share it with you when you have completed yours (C-6.2:2-3).

You can heal the entire world.

What would you do with all power? According to the Course, you would heal the world, so that there was no more war, no more crime, no one afraid and no unhappiness left on the face of the earth. This may sound completely outlandish, that one mind could heal the entire world. The author of the Course, however, makes this promise repeatedly. It is especially clear in this passage from *Psychotherapy: Purpose, Process and Practice*:

> One wholly egoless therapist could heal the world without a word, merely by being there. No one need see him or talk to him or even know of his existence. His simple Presence is enough to heal (P-2.III.3:7-9).

A common objection raised to this idea is that Jesus supposedly has all power in Heaven and earth, and *he* hasn't healed the world. But according to the Course, he has. He has healed all minds, has brought everyone to complete enlightenment. It is just taking a long time for this deep-level healing to work its way through our collective resistance and emerge on the surface.

These are magnificent promises, especially when you remember how badly you have wanted to make a difference, how often you have wanted to help a friend but have felt powerless to do so. As a true miracle worker, you *could* make a difference. You could bring about genuine miracles in the lives around you, as well as in lives you will never know about.

However, given that we have not taken hold of this power as yet, what does all of this mean for us now? What relevance does it have for us that *someday* we will be able to do this? The following passage provides the answer:

> Could you but realize for a single instant the power of healing that the reflection of God, shining in you, can bring to all the world, you could not wait to make the mirror of your mind clean to receive the image of the holiness that heals the world (T-14.IX.7:1).

If you only knew the healing power you could bring to the world, you couldn't wait to clean your mind and receive that power.

-10-
Accepting the Atonement for Oneself

by Allen

A *Course in Miracles* tells us, in seven to ten different places spanning the entire Course[1], that the sole responsibility of a miracle worker is to accept the Atonement for himself. In this final chapter, we are going to look closely at this topic, which is literally all-important (the *only* responsibility) for anyone who expects to achieve the Course's goal of becoming a miracle worker. We'll be looking at it under four headings:

- *The importance of accepting the Atonement*
- *The real meaning of accepting the Atonement*
- *The relationship between miracles and accepting the Atonement*
- *The purpose and results of accepting the Atonement*

It's difficult to separate these four topics from one another, so I am not really going to try to. I'll focus on each one, but as we go through passages for one topic, we'll pull out thoughts about some of the others as well.

The Importance of Accepting the Atonement

I have chosen what are, to me, the five most significant references about accepting the Atonement to consider in some detail. Let's look at each of these passages, and see what we can learn about why accepting the Atonement for oneself is so important.

The First Passage: T-2.V.5

The sole responsibility of the miracle worker is to accept the Atonement for himself. This means you recognize that mind is the only

---

[1]There are seven clear references to the concept: T-2.V.5:1, T-5.V.7:8, T-18.VII.1:4, T-25.IX.9:6, M-7.3:2, M-18.4:5, and M-22.1:10. There are three additional references that are not so clear-cut, but can easily be counted as less direct references: T-8.III.6:1-6, W-pII.337.1:4, and M-24.6:1-2.

creative level, and that its errors are healed by the Atonement. Once you accept this, your mind can only heal. By denying your mind any destructive potential and reinstating its purely constructive powers, you place yourself in a position to undo the level confusion of others. The message you then give to them is the truth that their minds are similarly constructive, and their miscreations cannot hurt them. By affirming this you release the mind from overevaluating its own learning device, and restore the mind to its true position as the learner (T-2.V.5:1-6).

This is the seminal passage in Chapter 2 of the Text, in which the principle is stated for the first time. The author has put the key sentence in italics, so let's pay close attention to it. First, let's simply be certain we understand its most obvious meaning, paying close attention to it to impress it on our minds.

"Sole" means "only" or "the only one of its kind." This is not simply the main or primary responsibility; it is the *only* responsibility. There is no other responsibility after this one.

The word "responsibility" denotes something we, as miracle workers, are required to do. It is a "response" that I am to make in any and every situation. What is that responsibility? It is to "accept" something.

The word "accept" is a passive word, not truly an active one. I accept a gift that is given to me. I accept the truth about a situation, instead of fighting against it. Something is offered or presented to me, and my responsibility is simply to accept or receive it.

And what is it I must accept? "The Atonement." Atonement is the healing of a split that never occurred, the principle that the separation never happened; to accept that for myself is to allow my own mind to be healed of its belief in that split, to accept my own mind's union with God's Mind. Recall that, just two paragraphs earlier (T-2.V.3:5), the Course tells us that in order to work miracles, we must be—however briefly—in our right mind. Accepting the Atonement means very much the same thing as being in my right mind. To work miracles I must be in my right mind; to work miracles, I must accept the Atonement.

Now recall that we have defined a miracle as the activity of the Holy Spirit that shifts our perception from false to true. That sounds an awful lot like what we've just said about accepting the Atonement, doesn't it? So accepting the Atonement for ourselves, and receiving the miracle, are also very much the same thing. To say that in order to work miracles we must receive the miracle and so be in our right mind, and to say that in order to work miracles we must accept the Atonement, are just different ways of saying the same thing.

The added element in this key saying is that accepting the Atonement for ourselves, or receiving the miracle, is the *only* part *we* are responsible for. It is up to us to choose to do it. We must be willing; we must invite the Holy Spirit to heal our minds. And that is *all* we are responsible for. From that point, He takes over. His activity heals us; that is the miracle. He then directs us in what to do or say, or where to go; He selects miracles for us to extend to others. And He does the actual extension; the Holy Spirit in our minds joins with the Holy Spirit in the minds of our brothers, and—if they are willing, just as we had to be willing—offers them the miracle, offers them the healing of their own minds.

Now, look at the second sentence: "This means you recognize that mind is the only creative level, and that its errors are healed by the Atonement." Here is another way of describing what accepting the Atonement means. To invite the Holy Spirit to heal our minds, we have to recognize that all cause is in the mind—not in behavior, not in external things, and not in other people, but in our own minds. We have to realize that the mind is all that needs healing, and that mind is healed by letting go of thoughts of separation and accepting our oneness with God and with each other. Once again, this parallels what is said about the miracle: The miracle is the result of bringing cause (our thoughts) together with its effects (our experiences in this world).

Third sentence: "Once you accept this, your mind can only heal." We need to read the next sentence as well to get the full implication of this: "By denying your mind any destructive potential and reinstating its purely constructive powers, you place yourself in a position to undo the level confusion of others." In other words, when you accept the Atonement, you are denying that your mind can destroy anything. You are recognizing that, whatever insane thoughts you have entertained, they have not broken your union with God or your brothers. You are accepting the fact that you have not sinned, and your wish for separation has had no real effects. You are realizing that your mind cannot threaten anything that is real, and therefore, all it *can* do is heal and bless. It is purely constructive in its powers, just as God's Mind is.

When we accept the Atonement, it corrects what these early Text sections call "level confusion." Level confusion asserts two false ideas that mix the body with the mind:

- that the body can and does affect the mind
- that the mind's mistaken thoughts can actually create real effects separate and apart from mind, which can turn to attack and harm us.

Atonement asserts the opposite of both of these ideas:

- that the body *cannot* affect the mind
- that ideas leave not their source, but remain in mind, where, as mistaken thoughts, they can be corrected.

In other words, your "errors" never really occurred; your mis-thoughts had no effect. Both accepting the Atonement and the miracle impart this same lesson. Basically, then, *accepting the Atonement for yourself is simply another way to describe receiving the miracle for yourself.* Thus, accepting the Atonement brings the realization that your errors have never occurred:

> The escape is brought about by your acceptance of the Atonement, which enables you to realize that your errors never really occurred (T-2.I.4:4).

Accepting the Atonement means realizing that mind cannot create *beyond itself.* This is the same thought as the statement, frequently repeated in the Course, "Ideas leave not their source" (W-pI.132.5:3, for instance). Therefore, the mistakes of the mind do not create anything real in the physical world; they only make illusions. Another way of saying the same thing is that we deny the destructive potential of our minds; they cannot actually destroy anything real.

The mention of undoing the level confusion *of others* is a definite reference to working miracles. In the preceding section of Chapter 2, it was stated that miracles are the means of correcting level confusion (T-2.IV.2:3), which simply means assisting others to accept the Atonement for themselves and to recognize that mind is the only creative level, and that mind alone needs to be healed.

The rest of the paragraph we are analyzing just recapitulates what miracle working is: We extend to others the lesson we have learned. Like our own mind, their minds are only constructive; they can only heal, "and their miscreations cannot hurt them" (T-2.V.5:5).

Summary: *The meaning of accepting the Atonement in this passage is:* accepting both the creative power of mind and the healing of mind's errors.

The main thought of the paragraph is: To extend a miracle to others I must first receive the miracle for myself.

The Second Passage: T-5.V.7

Accepting the Atonement frees us from thinking that we are responsible for the effects of our wrong thinking, because in reality they never occurred. Another long paragraph makes this point quite clearly:

> Irrational thought is disordered thought. God Himself orders your thought because your thought was created by Him. Guilt feelings are always a sign that you do not know this. They also show that you believe you can think apart from God, and want to. Every disor-

dered thought is attended by guilt at its inception, and maintained by guilt in its continuance. Guilt is inescapable by those who believe they order their own thoughts, and must therefore obey their dictates. This makes them feel responsible for their errors without recognizing that, by accepting this responsibility, they are reacting irresponsibly. If the sole responsibility of the miracle worker is to accept the Atonement for himself, and I assure you that it is, then the responsibility for <what> is atoned for cannot be yours. The dilemma cannot be resolved except by accepting the solution of undoing. You <would> be responsible for the effects of all your wrong thinking if it could not be undone. The purpose of the Atonement is to save the past in purified form only. If you accept the remedy for disordered thought, a remedy whose efficacy is beyond doubt, how can its symptoms remain? (T-5.V.7:1-12).

The message I want to glean out of this paragraph can be stated like this: If our *only* responsibility is accepting the Atonement, then we are *not* responsible for cleaning up our mistakes, or for the effects of all our wrong thinking. We are not responsible for trying to right all the wrongs we believe we have committed. That is the responsibility of the Holy Spirit, and He will do it if we do not interfere.

If we *were* responsible for the effects of our wrong thinking, we *would* be guilty. Guilt is often a result of realizing the truth that our thoughts have produced the world we see; we feel terribly guilty for making such a world. The Course is trying to head off our self-condemnation.

Another way of putting it is this: Our responsibility is to apply the remedy (the Atonement) to the cause (our thoughts); we need not concern ourselves with trying to fix all the effects, or symptoms of our thoughts. That includes, no doubt, such things as physical illness. If we accept the remedy for our thoughts, the symptoms of those thoughts cannot remain. The effects can be undone, and will be undone. Part of what accepting the Atonement means, then, is accepting that the undoing of the effects is His job, not ours. He may undo some of them through us; we may engage in restitution, in "making things right" in some external way, but only at His direction. And often, the things that seem most impossible to undo will be undone with no effort on our part at all. "I do not feel guilty, because the Holy Spirit will undo all the consequences of my wrong decision if I will let Him" (T-5.VII.6:10).

This is, for me, the central meaning of accepting the Atonement: allowing myself to be released from guilt for the wrongs I believe I have done. Only when I can be free from guilt, at least for a moment, can the miracle extend from my mind to release my brother from guilt.

Summary: *Our responsibility is to apply the remedy (the Atonement) to the cause (our thoughts); we need not concern ourselves with trying to fix all the effects, or symptoms of our thoughts, and we need not feel guilty.*

The Third Passage: T-8.III.6

This passage shows us that a part of accepting the Atonement is actually looking at our ego and its insane thoughts:

> The Kingdom cannot be found alone, and you who are the Kingdom cannot find yourself alone. To achieve the goal of the curriculum, then, you cannot listen to the ego, whose purpose is to defeat its own goal. The ego does not know this, because it does not know anything. But you can know it, and you will know it if you are willing to look at what the ego would make of you. This is your responsibility, because once you have really looked at it you will accept the Atonement for yourself. What other choice could you make? (T-8.III.6:1-6).

Here, we are being told that part of our responsibility is to "look at what the ego would make of you." This may seem at first to be something in addition to accepting the Atonement, but really it isn't. It is the *motivation* for accepting the Atonement, and actually part of that acceptance. Remember that accepting the Atonement involves seeing the mind as the only creative level. Looking at what the ego would make of you is nothing more than recognizing that the suffering you are experiencing is the effect of nothing but your own thoughts, when you listen to the ego. When you realize what you are doing to yourself, and see how undesirable it really is, you stop doing it; you accept your Self as God created you. You allow your thoughts to be healed by the Holy Spirit. That change of mind, realizing what you are doing to yourself and then choosing something different, is basically the same act as accepting the Atonement or receiving the miracle.

Summary: *Accepting the Atonement means realizing what you and your ego are doing to yourself, without guilt, and choosing something different.*

The Fourth Passage: M-7.2:8–3:11

This idea of not being responsible for removing the effects of wrong thinking applies even to the situation of offering miracles to others, when we may be inclined to think that our offer of a miracle has failed when the external symptoms do not immediately disappear. Even here, our only responsibility is having our own mind healed. It is fairly easy to see, in this context, why accepting the Atonement for himself is the only responsibility the miracle worker has:

> Having offered love, only love can be received. It is in this that the teacher of God must trust. This is what is really meant by the statement that the one responsibility of the miracle worker is to accept the Atonement for himself. The teacher of God is a miracle worker because he gives the gifts he has received. Yet he must first accept them. He need do no more, nor is there more that he could do. By accepting healing he can give it. If he doubts this, let him remember Who gave the gift and Who received it. Thus is his doubt corrected. He thought the gifts of God could be withdrawn. That was a mistake, but hardly one to stay with. And so the teacher of God can only recognize it for what it is, and let it be corrected for him (M-7.2:8-3:11).

This occurs in the section titled "Should Healing Be Repeated?" The idea here is that a miracle worker has offered healing to a brother, but the symptoms persist. Should he attempt to repeat the healing? The simple answer is, No. He has to learn to trust that if he offered love, then only love could be received. To doubt that the healing was given is actually to doubt that his own mind was healed when he gave it, and to doubt that the other person was up to receiving it. The remedy for that is, once again, accepting the Atonement for oneself! It is the healer's mind that needs healing, not the person whose symptoms are persisting. It is his mistaken thought that God's gifts could be withdrawn that needs correction. He has offered only love, and therefore only love could be received.

Summary: *Accepting the Atonement for yourself means not doubting the power of God's love in you to heal others.*

The Fifth Passage: M-18.4

> In order to heal, it thus becomes essential for the teacher of God to let all his own mistakes be corrected. If he senses even the faintest hint of irritation in himself as he responds to anyone, let him instantly realize that he has made an interpretation that is not true. Then let him turn within to his Eternal Guide, and let Him judge what the response should be. So is he healed, and in his healing is his pupil healed with him. The sole responsibility of God's teacher is to accept the Atonement for himself. Atonement means correction, or the undoing of errors. When this has been accomplished, the teacher of God becomes a miracle worker by definition. His

sins have been forgiven him, and he no longer condemns himself. How can he then condemn anyone? And who is there whom his forgiveness can fail to heal? (M-18.4:1-10).

This paragraph is from "How Is Correction Made?", which deals with how a teacher of God responds to "magic thoughts" in his pupil. It's really another example of the same kind of thing we saw about healing, only this time it deals with unhealed thoughts instead of unhealed behavior or unhealed bodies. It says much the same thing: The teacher's only responsibility is allowing his own thoughts to be corrected. He isn't responsible for trying to forcibly change his pupil's thinking, for instance, by direct argument. If he allows his own mind to be healed, ending his own self-condemnation ("I'm not a good teacher" might be one thought in his mind), then he can no longer condemn his pupil; and that forgiveness will bring healing to the pupil. "In his healing is his pupil healed with him."

This is why accepting the Atonement for himself is so important to the miracle worker. Only a healed mind can bring healing to another mind. Only a mind that forgives, that harbors no condemnation or judgment towards others, can offer healing, because *that is how healing is offered.*

Miracles are natural signs of forgiveness (T-1.I.21:1).

Through miracles you accept God's forgiveness by extending it to others (T-1.I.21:2).

Only forgiveness offers miracles (T-25.IX.8:5).

Forgiveness is the home of miracles (W-pII.13.3:1).

Summary: *Accepting the Atonement for yourself means letting the Holy Spirit heal your mind of judgments concerning others' mistaken thinking and your own seeming failure to reach them.*

The Real Meaning of Accepting the Atonement

We've seen so far that accepting the Atonement is similar to receiving the miracle for ourselves. It means recognizing that our thoughts are the cause and our experience and our world are the effects, and yet our mistaken thoughts are not a source of guilt because they have caused nothing *real*. Some of the other aspects of accepting the Atonement are:

Giving up disordered thoughts and accepting re-ordered thoughts

Your mind does make your future, and it will turn it back to full creation at any minute if it accepts the Atonement first. It will also return to full creation the instant it has done so. Having given up its disordered thought, the proper ordering of thought becomes quite apparent (T-5.V.8:6-8).

If you will recall, the Text defines the miracle in this way:

A miracle is a correction introduced into false thinking by me. It acts as a catalyst, breaking up erroneous perception and reorganizing it properly (T-1.I.37:1-2).

Accepting the Atonement and receiving a miracle are different words for the same thing; although one speaks of repairing disordered *thought* while the other speaks of breaking up erroneous *perception*, they are obviously speaking of the same healing transformation. We can say, therefore, that when we accept the Atonement, we receive the miracle.

Allowing our own thoughts to be healed enables us to become miracle workers because now our thinking does not lend support to the disordered thinking of others:

Accepting the Atonement for yourself means not to give support to someone's dream of sickness and of death. It means that you share not his wish to separate, and let him turn illusions on himself. Nor do you wish that they be turned, instead, on you. Thus have they no effects (T-28.IV.1:1-4).

Because you have accepted the Atonement, recognizing the mind as cause, and seeing that mind's miscreations are not real, you do not support the other person's misperceptions. You represent an alternative perception to him. You don't support the idea that his illusions can split off from his mind and turn on him, nor do you think that his illusions can turn on you. In that way, you show him that his mistakes have no effects, and therefore are not real.

Accepting your oneness with all of creation

Accepting the Atonement includes recognizing that you are a part of God's creation along with everything and everyone.

By accepting the Atonement for yourself, you are deciding against the belief that you can be alone, thus dispelling the idea of separation and affirming your true identification with the whole Kingdom as literally part of you (T-7.VIII.7:3).

If your "sins" are not real, but only mistaken thoughts, then you are not separate from God, and joined with Him you are joined to all of His creation. The separation never happened.

Accepting innocence and the end of guilt

One of the greatest meanings of accepting the Atonement for yourself, I believe, is that it means accepting your own sinlessness. We have already seen the basis for this: If our mistaken thoughts are only thoughts, with no real effect beyond the mind, then we cannot be guilty of sin. Only if our mis-thoughts have somehow left our minds and become separate from us, and real, could we be guilty. So accepting the Atonement includes accepting the end of guilt.

When you have accepted the Atonement for yourself, you will realize there is no guilt in God's Son (T-13.I.6:1).

Clearly, accepting Atonement means the end of our guilt.

If, then, you offer blessing, it must have come first to yourself. And you must also have accepted it as yours, for how else could you give it away? That is why miracles offer you the testimony that you are blessed. If what you offer is complete forgiveness you must have let guilt go, accepting the Atonement for yourself and learning you are guiltless. How could you learn what has been done for you, unknown to you, unless you do what you would have to do if it had been done for you? (T-14.I.1:4-8).

We see here that accepting the Atonement means letting guilt go, and learning that you are guiltless. But this adds a very important aspect, one we have seen before with the miracle: It states the two sides of a paradox. You cannot give away guiltlessness unless you have received it for yourself. "If what you offer is complete forgiveness you must have let guilt go." And yet, you may not *recognize* that you have done this! And the way that you "learn what has been done for you, *unknown to you*," is by doing "what you would have to do if it *had* been done for you." That is, you release others from guilt by forgiving, because that is "what you would have to do" if *you* have been forgiven and released from your own guilt; and, *as you forgive others*, you finally recognize the reality of your own forgiveness. In other words, "You accept forgiveness as accomplished in yourself when you forgive" (W-159.2:2).

> *I choose to testify to my acceptance of the
> Atonement, not to its rejection.
> I would accept my guiltlessness by making it
> manifest and sharing it* (T-14.III.3:7-8).

That's an interesting choice of words: you "testify to your acceptance of the Atonement" by "making it manifest and sharing it." You *demonstrate* that you have accepted the Atonement by forgiving others, by sharing guiltlessness with them. You "do what you would have to do if it *had* been done for you," and that is how you learn that it *has* been done for you.

The Relationship Between Miracles and Accepting the Atonement

I think by now that we can see clearly how miracles relate to accepting the Atonement. Accepting the Atonement is the precondition for *giving* miracles, and is virtually identical with *receiving* the miracle for yourself. Accepting the Atonement means allowing the Holy Spirit to perform a miracle in your mind, breaking up your disordered thinking and replacing it with His own thoughts and perceptions. This places you in your right mind, and from that place, you are able to offer miracles to others.

Yet it seems that your accepting the Atonement and being placed in your right mind can happen in a way that is "unknown to you." You have done it but you don't fully realize it, and the way that you come to cement your acceptance and make it real to yourself is by manifesting it, which you do by sharing it. You offer miracles to others, and so *confirm* the reality of the miracle in your own mind.

The Results of Accepting the Atonement

If accepting the Atonement and receiving the miracle are virtually identical, then we would expect that their results will be alike as well. And many of them are.

In closing, let me provide a summarized list of what results from accepting the Atonement (or receiving the miracle). For the full effect, look up the reference for each point. Let yourself take a few moments to envision each of these points becoming true of yourself!

- The Atonement will radiate from you to everyone the Holy Spirit sends you (T-12.VII.1:5).
- Accepting the Atonement ends the false sense of separation from God (T-13.In.2:1; W-pI.139.9:6-10:2).
- Accepting the Atonement ends guilt in you and in your brother (T-14.III.7:1-7).
- Accepting the Atonement teaches you what immortality is (T-13.I.9:1).
- Accepting the Atonement teaches that the past has never been and the future will not be (T-13.I.9:1).
- Accepting the Atonement brings about escape from the past and total lack of interest in the future (M-24.6:3).
- Accepting the Atonement gives us faith to offer healing and forgiveness to others (T-19.I.9:1-7).
- Accepting the Atonement for yourself lets you accept the correction of your brother's errors (M-6.1:4-5).
- Accepting the Atonement brings physical healing, and allows you to heal everything and offer every miracle (M-22.1:5-12,6:10-14).
- Accepting the Atonement lets you look on the fear of God unterrified (T-19.IV(D).9:1).
- Accepting the Atonement for myself will save the entire world (W-pII.297.1:1-4; M-23.2:1).
- Accepting the Atonement for myself will bring me:
    - perfect peace
    - eternal safety
    - everlasting love
    - freedom from all thought of loss
    - complete deliverance from suffering
    - undiluted happiness
    - the sense of God's Love protecting me
    - the understanding that God loves His Son
    - the knowledge that I am the Son my Father loves (W-pII.337).

You are entitled to miracles because of what you are.
You will receive miracles because of what God is.
And you will offer miracles because you are
one with God (W-pI.77.1:1-3).

THE CIRCLE OF ATONEMENT:
Teaching and Healing Center
is a non-profit, tax-exempt corporation founded in 1993, and is located in Sedona, Arizona. It is based on *A Course in Miracles*, the three-volume modern spiritual classic, which we believe was authored by Jesus through a human scribe.

OUR MISSION STATEMENT
To discern the author's vision of A Course in Miracles *and manifest that in our lives, in the lives of students, and in the world.*

A CLOSER LOOK AT THIS VISION
The Circle's purpose is to serve students of the Course as they walk its path of spiritual development. We see this manifesting through the following four points:

1. TO FAITHFULLY DISCERN THE AUTHOR'S VISION OF *A COURSE IN MIRACLES*.
• In our interpreting of the Course to strive for total fidelity to its words and their intended meaning, regardless of what we want those words to mean or not to mean, regardless of whether they differ with what we believe or have been taught, regardless even of whether we end up agreeing with them.

• To thereby discover the Course as the author saw it, to uncover the thought system he placed in it and the program he designed for realizing that thought system.

2. TO BE AN INSTRUMENT IN JESUS' PLAN TO MANIFEST HIS VISION OF THE COURSE IN THE LIVES OF HIS STUDENTS AND IN THE WORLD.
• To see Jesus as the teacher and guide of the Circle; to see ourselves as instruments in his plan and to follow his guidance in all that we do.

• To do what we can to help the Course get started on the right foot here at the beginning of its history.

• To do our best to communicate to students and ground in the world the understanding of the Course's thought system that Jesus intended.

• To do our best to ground in the world and in the lives of students the intended use of the Course as a literal program in true spiritual awakening.

3. TO HELP SPARK AN ENDURING TRADITION BASED ENTIRELY ON STUDENTS JOINING TOGETHER IN DOING THE COURSE AS THE AUTHOR ENVISIONED.

• To help spark a global support system phenomenon, by first cultivating one in Sedona and then by helping others establish support systems in other areas.

• To help the Course become an ongoing spiritual tradition, a tradition totally based on understanding and using the Course as the author intended.

4. TO BECOME AN EMBODIMENT, A BIRTHPLACE OF WHAT WE WANT TO SEE HAPPEN IN THE WORLD.

• For those of us in the Circle to follow *A Course in Miracles* as our individual path; to learn forgiveness through its program.

• For those of us in the Circle to join with each other in a group holy relationship based on the common goal of awakening to God through study, practice, and extension of the principles in *A Course in Miracles*.

• To join with other individuals, groups, and centers that feel the same calling.

• To have a facility in Sedona that would be the home of our work. This facility will most likely eventually include three general aspects or wings:

  • *The Teaching Wing*: Communicating the thought system and program of the Course.
  • *The Support Wing*: Supporting students in doing the Course, in the study, practice, and extension of the Course.
  • *The Healing Wing*: Becoming proficient in the Course's unique approach to healing, extending healing to others, and training others in doing so.

• To spark a local support system in Sedona that could be a pilot program for support systems elsewhere in the world.

• To, as individuals, as a group, as a center, and as a local Course support culture, become a seed for an ongoing spiritual tradition based on *A Course in Miracles*. ✳ ✳ ✳

FRIENDS OF THE CIRCLE

We invite you to look within to discern your place in this vision. Does it speak to you in some way? Do you feel a resonance with any part of it? Please see the next page for more information on how you may become a "Friend of the Circle," joining us in a common purpose.

Friends of the Circle
Joining in a Common Vision

If the vision of the Circle presented here speaks to you, we invite you to join with us in it. Ask yourself: Is this a vision I want to see promulgated in the world? Is this something I want to give my support to? If so, perhaps you would like to become a "Friend of the Circle." Benefits include:

Category 1: $60.00 per year*
- Four-issue subscription to our newsletter, *A Better Way*
- Updates and special reports every other month or so, making you an informed partner
- Support from one of our staff in your study and application of the Course
- Special materials and hand-outs on support groups, Text studies, responses to questions
- Feedback forms to give us your ideas and concerns
- Join us in our daily Workbook and meditation practice

Category 2: $130.00 per year* - Includes all of the above, plus
- Four upcoming products, valued at a total of $70.00
  (including book rate shipping fees)

Quarterly payment plans are available for both categories, at a slightly higher cost.

*ALL PRICES ARE FOR U.S. ONLY, and are subject to change. Please contact The Circle of Atonement at (520) 282-0790 for the most current information.

TO BECOME A FRIEND OF THE CIRCLE
- *Confirm the current price for the category membership you desire with the Circle.*
- *Write us a paragraph or two about why you want to become a Friend. What about this speaks to you?*
- *Take a few moments to silently join with us in purpose.*
- *Enclose your initial payment/donation (If you are unable to afford the amount listed, see our Financial Policy).*

SERVICES CURRENTLY OFFERED

NEWSLETTER, BOOKS, AND BOOKLETS

A BETTER WAY is the Circle's newsletter, published quarterly. It is primarily a teaching journal, containing articles by Robert, Allen, and others, on the Course.

Our other publications, ranging in size from 44-page booklets to full-size books, are available in bookstores or directly from The Circle of Atonement. Books are published quarterly, in between the newsletters, and are expositions of a theme or section from the Course.

THE LEARNING CIRCLE

This is our school for students of the Course, and is a division of the Teaching Wing. It is designed to aid students in their reading, study, and understanding of the Course. The school, started in 1994, consists of introductory classes, Text study classes, and topical classes. Classes are available by correspondence following the in-person presentation of the class. Additional information is available by requesting our introductory packet from the Ordering Information page.

WORKSHOPS, SEMINARS AND RETREATS

The Circle currently offers workshops, seminars and retreats in Sedona. These are open to all individuals interested in *A Course in Miracles*. Dates and specifics are announced in every newsletter mailing (or call the Circle for more information and dates of events). Robert and Allen are available to speak at other locations by invitation.

SUPPORT SYSTEM

The Circle is currently developing a multi-faceted support system in Sedona, under the direction of Jeanne Cashin and Robert Perry. Currently in place are Support Meetings, designed to encourage sharing of how we apply Course principles to our lives, as well as difficulties we have in doing so; Workbook Support Meetings and Meditation Meetings, designed to facilitate the practice of the Lessons; one-on-one support for local students, as well as telephone support for students outside the local area. See Issue #18 of *A Better Way* for more information.

TEACHERS

Robert Perry began teaching in 1986 at Miracle Distribution Center in California. He has written the popular *An Introduction to 'A Course in Miracles,'* as well as *The Elder Brother: Jesus in 'A Course in Miracles.'* Robert is the President of The Circle of Atonement, as well as teacher and staff writer, and has lectured extensively in the U.S. and abroad.

Allen Watson is a member of the Board of Directors of the Circle, as well as writer and teacher. He has written a number of booklets, including *A Healed Mind Does Not Plan* and *What Is Death?,* and the *A Workbook Companion* series on the Internet and in book form. Before moving to Sedona, he published the *Miracle Thoughts* newsletter and led Course study groups in New Jersey.

* * *

FINANCIAL POLICY

The Circle is supported entirely by your purchases and gifts. We encourage you to give, not in payment for goods received, but in support of our present and future outreach. No one will be refused if they cannot pay. If you would like any of our materials or services and cannot afford it, then:

- write us a note saying so
- and give what you are able

We ask you to look within to see if you might be led to support the Circle's vision financially with a donation above the list price of materials. Please note that only amounts given *over* the list price are considered tax-deductible.

Please see *A Better Way,* Issue #18 for a more detailed explanation.

THE VISION OF THE LEARNING CIRCLE

Our vision is to aid students in their personal study of the Course. Since the Course is a book, the foundational activity for any student is simply reading the book. This is doubly so for this particular course, for it makes the study and understanding of its thought system the foundation for walking its path. As the opening line of the Workbook says, "A theoretical foundation such as the text provides is necessary as a framework to make the exercises in this workbook meaningful."

Based on the above, *that* one reads the book, *how* one reads the book, and *how much* one understands its thought system are all crucial. All of these provide a foundation for giving meaning to the application of the Course. The purpose of The Learning Circle is to aid and support students in all of the above things:
- in reading the book
- in reading it in a way that mines its treasures
- in understanding what it says
- in seeing how this understanding applies in our lives.

Our experience has been that this reading, study and understanding are indeed the foundation for the entire path of the Course. As students become more firmly grounded in this, their experience of the Course and their ability to apply it increase exponentially.

THE CORRESPONDENCE SCHOOL

If you are unable to attend the classes offered in person, and wish to participate in The Learning Circle program, the tape sets from the classes are available as correspondence classes. Each correspondence class consists of a reading list, a study guide, student feedback forms, and student-teacher interaction via phone, e-mail, tape recording and or writing. At the completion of a correspondence class, the student receives a certificate of completion from The Learning Circle.

Two of our correspondence class tape sets, 101 and 102, serve as prerequisites for continuing study with The Learning Circle, either through correspondence classes or in-person seminars. For more information, please request our information packet, which outlines the school program and class offerings (see Ordering Information page).

Subscription Information for
A Better Way Newsletter

A Better Way is designed as a teaching journal for students of the Course. The suggested subscription price is $10.00* for four (4) quarterly issues (for more information, please see the financial policy).

Back Newsletter Issues of *A Better Way*

(available as of this printing)
Price for each newsletter copy: $2.00*
(Christmas issues: $.50)*

An Introduction to *A Course in Miracles*-- Perry; A brief overview of the Course; 44 pp.; *$2.00**

ACIM Interpretive Forum
"Prosperity and *A Course in Miracles*"

With Position Papers by Allen Watson and Tony Ponticello, and Response Papers by several participants, this journal seeks to explore the Course's position on material abundance and divine supply.; 47 pp.; $5.00*

A list of *Reprinted Articles* by Allen Watson and Robert Perry from other Course-based publications is available upon request. Please mark your interest on the Ordering Information page.

*ALL PRICES ARE FOR U.S. ONLY, and are subject to change. Please contact the Circle directly for the most current information.

Books & Booklets based on
A Course in Miracles

#1 Seeing the Face of Christ in All Our Brothers -- Perry
Learning how to see the Divine in everyone; 47 pp.; *$5.00**

#2 *NO LONGER IN PRINT (see #18)*

#3 Shrouded Vaults of the Mind -- Perry
A tour through the many levels of the human mind; 44 pp.; *$5.00**

#4 Guidance: Living the Inspired Life -- Perry; A practical manual
for receiving and discerning guidance; 44 pp.; *$5.00**

#5 *NO LONGER IN PRINT (see #18)*

#6 Reality & Illusion: An Overview of Course Metaphysics Part I
-- Perry; The Course's view of what is truly real; 44 pp.; *$5.00**

**#7 Reality & Illusion: An Overview of Course Metaphysics Part
II --** Perry; The Course's view of what is truly real; 52 pp.; *$5.00**

#8 A Healed Mind Does Not Plan -- Watson
Allowing God into your plan-making; 40 pp.; *$5.00**

#9 Through Fear to Love -- Watson
Explores the fear of looking within; 44 pp.; *$5.00**

#10 The Journey Home -- Watson; A sequential description of the
spiritual journey as seen in the Course; 64 pp.; *$5.00**

**#11 Everything You Always Wanted to Know About
JUDGMENT But Were Too Busy Doing It to Notice --**
Perry & Watson; The nature of judgment and its relinquishment;
59 pp.; *$5.00**

#12 The Certainty of Salvation -- Perry & Watson; Answers our
doubts that we will make it home to God; 51 pp.; *$5.00**

#13 What Is Death? -- Watson
The Course's view of what death really is; 42 pp.; *$5.00**

#14 The Workbook as a Spiritual Practice -- Perry;
A guide for getting the most out of the Workbook; 57 pp.; *$5.00**

***ALL PRICES ARE FOR U.S. ONLY, and are subject to change.
Please contact the Circle directly for the most current information.**

#15 I Need Do Nothing -- Watson;
A careful examination of one of the most empowering--and most misunderstood--sections of the Course; 57 pp.; *$5.00**

#16 A Course Glossary -- Perry; A detailed definition of over 150 terms from the Course; 96 pp; perfect-bound; *$7.00**

#17 Seeing the Bible Differently: How *A Course in Miracles* Views the Bible -- Watson; A look at the similarities and the differences, and the Course's own attitude toward the Bible; 80 pp.; perfect-bound; *$6.00**

#18 Relationships as a Spiritual Journey: From Specialness to Holiness -- Perry; An updated and revised combined edition of the most popular booklets in our series (#2 and #5) on special and holy relationships; 192 pp.; perfect-bound; *$10.00**

A Workbook Companion
**Commentaries on the *Workbook for Students* from
*A Course in Miracles***
by Allen Watson and Robert Perry

A three-volume set designed to aid students of the Course in their practice and understanding of the Workbook's daily lessons. Each volume includes a commentary and a practice summary of each lesson, as well as periodic overviews of the training goals of various lessons. These are not a replacement of the lessons themselves, but are rather a companion, with explanations, personal anecdotes, and advice on how to carry out the lessons. Each volume is perfect-bound.

Volume I -- covers Lessons 1 - 120 (320 pp.)   *$16.00**
Volume II -- covers Lessons 121 - 243 (304 pp.)   *$16.00**
Volume III -- covers Lessons 244 - 365 (352 pp.)   *$18.00**

Tape Sets from
The Learning Circle

The unedited live classes given in Sedona for students participating in our school are available on audio tape. If you are simply interested in listening to the classes, but not participating in the school, you may order the tape sets (and study guides, if desired), which are described below.

STUDY GUIDES $ 10.00*

Study guides are available for use with all tape sets except 101. Each study guide can be used alone or in connection with its corresponding tape set. All study guides are $10.00* each. When ordering, please be sure to specify the tape set number for which you want a study guide.

101 Basic Introduction to *A Course in Miracles* - 6 60-min. tapes $ 30.00*
For familiarizing students with the perspective of the Circle's instructors; offers an overview of the Course's message & thought system; the Course as a spiritual path; and more; Watson

**102 Bringing the Course to Life: Turning Study
Into Experience - 8 90-min. tapes** $ 40.00*
An intensive focusing on methods and techniques for studying the Course, taking into consideration its unique presentation of its thought system; Perry & Watson

TEXT STUDY SERIES

A detailed paragraph-by-paragraph study of the chapters specified.

201 Text Study, Chapters 1 - 3   10 90-minute tapes $ 60.00*
1: The Meaning of Miracles; 2: The Separation and the Atonement; 3: The Innocent Perception; Watson

202 Text Study, Chapters 4 - 6   10 90-minute tapes $ 60.00*
4: The Illusions of the Ego; 5: Healing and Wholeness; 6: The Lessons of Love; Perry & Watson

203 Text Study, Chapters 7 - 8   10 90-minute tapes $ 60.00*
7: The Gifts of the Kingdom; 8: The Journey Back; Perry & Watson

204 Text Study, Chapters 9 - 11   10 90-minute tapes $ 60.00*
9: The Acceptance of the Atonement; 10: The Idols of Sickness; 11: God or the Ego; Perry & Watson

*ALL PRICES ARE FOR U.S. ONLY, and are subject to change. Please contact the Circle directly for the most current information.

TOPICAL STUDY SERIES

Each tape set focuses on a particular theme derived from the Course,
determined to be of interest or a keynote for understanding.

301 Perception and Vision   10 90-minute tapes $ 60.00*
Includes: Projection makes perception; true perception & vision; dream roles &
shadow figures; Holy Spirit's interpretation; eyes of the body & eyes of Christ; Perry

302 The Holy Instant   10 90-minute tapes $ 60.00*
Includes a focus on chapter 15 of the Text; Perry & Watson

303 Judgment   10 90-minute tapes $ 60.00*
Includes study of what judgment really is; how the Holy Spirit uses judgment;
how we can release it; and more; Perry & Watson

304 The Certainty of Salvation   10 90-minute tapes $ 60.00*
Includes the what's, why's, and how's of salvation; our nature and the journey;
God's changelessness; the happy learner; who walks with us?; Perry & Watson

* * * * *

ORDERING INFORMATION

All publications and products listed previously are available as of this printing. ALL PRICES ARE FOR U.S. ONLY, and are subject to change. In addition, new titles become available each quarter; therefore, please contact the Circle directly for the most current information.

Information is available by writing or calling us at:

The Circle of Atonement: Teaching and Healing Center
P.O. Box 4238   W. Sedona, AZ 86340

Phone: (520) 282-0790   Fax: (520) 282-0523

In the U.S. toll-free: (888) 357-7520 (for orders only)

e-mail: circleofa@sedona.net

Or

You can learn more and order materials directly from our website at http://nen.sedona.net/circleofa/

Or

You can send the form below to the above address with your information:

*NAME*_____

*ADDRESS*_____

*CITY*_____   *PROVINCE/STATE*_____

*COUNTRY*_____   *POSTAL/ZIP CODE*_____

*PHONE*_____

_____ **PLEASE SEND ME A PACKET INCLUDING INFORMATION ON CURRENT PRODUCTS, NEWSLETTER SUBSCRIPTIONS, THE LEARNING CIRCLE PROGRAM, AND FRIENDS OF THE CIRCLE MEMBERSHIP**

_____ **PLEASE SEND ME A FREE LIST OF REPRINTED ARTICLES**